Learning WatchKit Programming

Second Edition

Learning WatchKit Programming

A Hands-On Guide to Creating watchOS 2 Applications

Second Edition

Wei-Meng Lee

Addison-Wesley

Boston • Columbus • Indianapolis • New York • San Francisco • Amsterdam • Cape Town
Dubai • London • Madrid • Milan • Munich • Paris • Montreal • Toronto • Delhi • Mexico City
Sao Paulo • Sidney • Hong Kong • Seoul • Singapore • Taipei • Tokyo

For information about buying this title in bulk quantities, or for special sales opportunities (which may include electronic versions; custom cover designs; and content particular to your business, training goals, marketing focus, or branding interests), please contact our corporate sales department at corpsales@pearsoned.com or (800) 382-3419.

For government sales inquiries, please contact governmentsales@pearsoned.com.

For questions about sales outside the United States, please contact international@pearsoned.com.

Visit us on the Web: informit.com/aw

Library of Congress Control Number: 2015952426

ISBN-13: 978-0-13-439898-3
ISBN-10: 0-13-439898-X

Text printed in the United States on recycled paper at RR Donnelley in Crawfordsville, Indiana.
First printing, December 2015

Editor-in-Chief
Mark L. Taub

Senior Acquisitions Editor
Trina MacDonald

Development Editor
Sheri Replin

Managing Editor
John Fuller

Full-Service Production Manager
Julie B. Nahil

Copy Editor
Barbara Wood

Indexer
Jack Lewis

Proofreader
Anna Popick

Technical Reviewers
Mark H. Granoff
Chaim Krause
Niklas Saers

Editorial Assistant
Olivia Basegio

Cover Designer
Chuti Prasertsith

Compositor
The CIP Group

❖

I dedicate this book with love to my family, and to my dearest wife,
who has had to endure my irregular work schedule and take care
of things while I was trying to meet writing deadlines!

❖

Contents at a Glance

Contents

Preface

Welcome to *Learning WatchKit Programming, Second Edition*!

This is an exciting time to be a programmer, as we are witnessing a new era of wearables. Although the Apple Watch is not the first wearable device in the market, its launch signified the intention of Apple to enter the wearable market in a big way. After successfully changing various industries—music, computer, phone, and mobile computing—Apple looks set to change the wearable industry. And nobody is taking this lightly.

As with the iPhone, much of the usefulness and functionality of the Apple Watch device actually come from the creativity of the third-party developers. In the early days of the iPhone, Apple restricted all third-party apps to web applications, as it wanted to retain the monopoly on developing natively for the device. However, due to the overwhelming protests of developers, Apple finally relented by releasing an SDK to support third-party apps. It was this decision that changed the fate of the iPhone; the iPhone would never have been so successful without the ability to support third-party apps.

When the Apple Watch was announced, Apple was quick to learn its lesson and realized that the success of the Apple Watch largely depends on the availability of apps that support it. Hence, before the release of the Apple Watch, the SDK was made available to developers to have a hand in developing Apple Watch apps.

Barely two months after the Apple Watch was made available for sale, Apple announced the second version of the Apple Watch OS, aptly named watchOS 2. Unsurprisingly, watchOS 2 now supports native apps and comes with a slew of new features.

The book you are holding in your hands right now (or reading on your phone or tablet) is a collection of tutorials that help you navigate the jungle of Apple Watch programming. This book contains all the fundamental topics that you need to get started in Apple Watch programming. In particular, this second edition has been fully updated to cover watchOS 2 programming.

Because this is a book on Apple Watch programming, I make a couple of assumptions about you, the reader:

- You should already be familiar with the basics of developing an iOS application. In particular, concepts like outlets and actions should not be new to you.
- You should be comfortable with the Swift programming language, but see the next section on how to get started with Swift if you are new to it.

What You'll Need

To get the most out of this book, note the following:

- You need a Mac, together with **Xcode**.
- Your Mac should be running at least **Mac OS X Yosemite (v10.10)** or later.
- You can download the latest version of Xcode from the Mac App Store. All of the code samples for this book have been tested against Xcode 7.
- If you plan to test your apps on a real device, you need to register to become a paying Apple developer (https://developer.apple.com/programs/). The program costs $99 per year for individuals. Once registered, you can register your Apple Watch's UDID with Apple (necessary for testing on Apple Watch). The Apple Watch works only with iPhone 5, iPhone 5c, iPhone 5s, iPhone 6, iPhone 6 Plus, iPhone 6s, and iPhone 6s Plus (or newer versions of the iPhones).
- Most of the code samples in this book can be tested and run on the iPhone Simulator without the need for a real device or Apple Watch. However, for some code examples, you need access to a real Apple Watch (for example, to access the hardware features like accelerometer, microphone, etc.).
- A number of examples in this book require an Internet connection in order to work, so ensure that you have an Internet connection when trying out the examples.
- All of the examples in this book are written in Swift 2.0. If you are not familiar with Swift, you can refer to Apple's web page on Swift at https://developer.apple.com/swift/resources/.

How This Book Is Organized

This book is styled as a tutorial. You try out the examples as I explain the concepts. This is a proven way to learn a new technology, and I strongly encourage you to type in the code as you work on the examples.

- **Chapter 1, "Getting Started with WatchKit Programming"**: In this chapter, you learn about the architecture of Apple Watch applications and how it ties in with your iOS apps. Most importantly, you get your chance to write a simple Apple Watch app and deploy it onto the Apple Watch Simulator.
- **Chapter 2, "Apple Watch Interface Navigation"**: In this chapter, you dive deeper into how your Apple Watch application navigates between multiple screens. You get to see how data is passed between screens and how to customize the look and feel of each screen.

- **Chapter 3, "Responding to User Actions"**: Designing the user interface (UI) for your Apple Watch application is similar to designing for iPhone apps. However, space is at a premium on the Apple Watch, and every millimeter on the screen must be put to good use in order to convey the exact intention of your app. In this chapter, you learn how to use the various UI controls in the Apple Watch to build your application. You will start off with the controls with which the user interacts.

- **Chapter 4, "Displaying and Gathering Information"**: While Chapter 3 covers the various controls with which the user interacts through the tap gesture, this chapter continues to explore the various controls available in the WatchKit framework, focusing on controls that display information, as well as controls that gather information.

- **Chapter 5, "Accessing the Apple Watch Hardware"**: In watchOS 1, Apple did not provide third-party developers access to the various hardware features of the Apple Watch, such as accelerometer, microphone, and Taptic Engine. However, in watchOS 2, Apple has exposed some of these features to developers so that they can create more exciting watch apps. In this chapter, you learn how to access some of these hardware features and see how they can be useful to the apps you are building.

- **Chapter 6, "Programming Complications"**: A complication is a function on a timepiece that does more than just tell the time. Complications on a timepiece include alarms, tachymeters, chronographs, calendars, and so on. In watchOS 2, third-party apps can now also display data in watch face complications. In this chapter, you learn the process of creating an application that displays complication data.

- **Chapter 7, "Interfacing with iOS Apps"**: This chapter discusses the Watch Connectivity Framework, a set of APIs that allow the containing iOS app to communicate with the watch app (and vice versa). In addition to discussing how apps intercommunicate, this chapter also discusses how to use location services in your watch app, as well as how to consume web services. Last, but not least, this chapter ends with a discussion on persisting data on your watch.

- **Chapter 8, "Displaying Notifications"**: In this chapter, you learn how to display notifications on your Apple Watch. Notifications received by the iPhone are sent to the Apple Watch, and you have the chance to customize the notifications so that you can display their essence quickly to the user.

- **Chapter 9, "Displaying Glances"**: Glances on the Apple Watch provide the user a quick way to gather information from apps. For example, Instagram's glance on the Apple Watch may show the most recently shared photo, and Twitter may show the latest trending tweets. In this chapter, you learn how to implement glances for your own apps.

About the Sample Code

The code samples in this book are written to provide the simplest way to understand core concepts without getting bogged down with details like beautifying the UI or detailed error checking. The philosophy is to convey key ideas in the simplest manner possible. In real-life apps, you are expected to perform detailed error handling and to create a user-friendly UI for your apps. Although I do provide several scenarios in which a certain concept is useful, it is ultimately up to you, the reader, to exercise your creativity to put the concepts to work, and perhaps create the next killer app.

Getting the Sample Code

To download the sample code used in this book, visit the book's web page on informIT.com at http://informit.com/title/9780134398983, click the **Extras** tab, and register your book.

Contacting the Author

If you have any comments or questions about this book, drop me an email at weimenglee@learn2develop.net, or stop by my web site at http://learn2develop.net.

Acknowledgments

Writing a book on emerging technology is always an exciting and perilous journey. On one end, you are dealing with the latest developments, going where not many have ventured, and on the other end you are dealing with many unknowns. To endure this journey, you need a lot of help and family support. I want to take this opportunity to thank the people who make all this happen.

I am indebted to Trina MacDonald, senior acquisitions editor at Pearson, for giving me the chance to work on this book. She has always been supportive of my proposals for new titles, and I am really glad that we have the chance to work together on this project. Thank you very much for the opportunity and guidance, Trina! I hope I did not disappoint you.

I want to thank the many heroes working behind the scenes—copy editor Barbara Wood; production editor Julie Nahil; and technical reviewers Mark H. Granoff, Chaim Krause, and Niklas Saers—for turning the manuscript into a book that I am proud of!

Last, but not least, I want to thank my family for all the support that they have always given me. Without their encouragement, this book would never have been possible.

About the Author

Wei-Meng Lee is a technologist and founder of Developer Learning Solutions (http://learn2develop.net), a technology company specializing in hands-on training on the latest web and mobile technologies. Wei-Meng speaks regularly at international conferences and has authored and coauthored numerous books on .NET, XML, Android, and iOS technologies. He writes extensively for informIT.com and mobiForge.com.

Getting Started with WatchKit Programming

Design is a funny word. Some people think design means how it looks. But of course, if you dig deeper, it's really how it works.

Steve Jobs

Apple Watch is a smartwatch created by Apple and officially announced by Tim Cook during the September 9, 2014, Apple event. It is touted as the next big thing after the launch of the iPhone and the iPad, and is expected to change the rules of wearables (just as the iPhone changed the smartphone industry and the iPad changed the tablet industry).

The Apple Watch runs on the watchOS operating system, which is based on iOS. The original watchOS 1.0 was released on April 24, 2015, along with the Apple Watch. Barely two months after its release, Apple announced the next version of watchOS at WWDC2015 (World Wide Developers Conference): watchOS 2. With watchOS 2, developers are now able to write native watch apps that run independently of the iPhone and are able to make use of the hardware features on the watch.

In this chapter, you learn about the architecture of Apple Watch applications and how they tie in with your iOS apps. Most importantly, you get your hands dirty by writing a simple Apple Watch app and deploying it onto the simulator.

Specifications of the Apple Watch

The Apple Watch is powered using a custom chip (dubbed the S1) from Apple. The back of the Apple Watch is a heart rate sensor, which is a set of LEDs and photodiodes mounted in a ceramic cover. The watch also has an accelerometer, WiFi, Bluetooth Low Energy (LE), and GPS. It is charged wirelessly using a magnetic charger, which snaps to the back of the watch.

The Apple Watch comes in two sizes (see Figure 1.1):

- **38mm watch (small)**: Resolution of 272 pixels by 340 pixels
- **42mm watch (large)**: Resolution of 312 pixels by 390 pixels

340   390

272   312

Figure 1.1   The resolutions of the Apple Watch sizes

To interact with the Apple Watch, you can use the following:

- **Digital Crown**: Allows you to scroll through lists of items, as well as zoom in or out of images, etc. The Digital Crown also acts as a Home button—pressing it returns you to the Home screen.
- **Force Touch**: A pressure-sensitive touchscreen, allowing it to tell the difference between a tap and a press.
- **Taptic Engine**: A haptic feedback system, which taps on your wrist to inform you of notifications and vibrates when you rotate the Digital Crown.

Getting the Tools for Development

To develop Apple Watch applications for watchOS 2, you need Xcode 7 or later, which you can download from the Mac App Store.

Xcode 7

The examples in this book were written and tested using Xcode 7. At the time of writing, Xcode 7 is in beta. Hence, you should expect to see some minor changes in screenshots in this book when the final release of Xcode 7 is available.

Xcode 7 contains the WatchKit framework that is used to create Apple Watch applications. In addition, Xcode 7 also comes with the Apple Watch Simulator, which allows you to test your Apple Watch application without using a real device.

What Is WatchKit?

WatchKit is a framework (similar to other frameworks such as CoreLocation or MapKit, for those of you familiar with iOS development) that contains all the classes that are necessary to create Apple Watch applications.

Understanding the WatchKit App Architecture

An Apple Watch application consists of three components (technically known as *bundles*):

- A **containing iOS** app that is used to install the Apple Watch application through the iPhone
- A **WatchKit app** containing the UI of the watch application
- A **WatchKit Extension** containing the code of the watch application

Note

The Apple Watch is compatible with iPhone 5, iPhone 5c, iPhone 5s, iPhone 6, iPhone 6 Plus, iPhone 6s, and iPhone 6s Plus running iOS 8.3 or later.

In watchOS 1.x, the WatchKit Extension (the application logic of your watch app) is hosted within the containing iOS app running on the iPhone (see Figure 1.2). The UI of your watch app is on the Apple Watch itself. This execution model is limited, as all interactions with the watch app must be communicated back to the iPhone, and hence the watch itself has this inherent reliance on the iPhone in order to work. This architecture has resulted in users reporting that first-generation watch apps were sluggish and took a long time to load.

Note

The iPhone and the Apple Watch communicate with each other using a Bluetooth LE (Low Energy) connection. The WatchKit framework encapsulates all the communication details, and it is totally transparent to the developer.

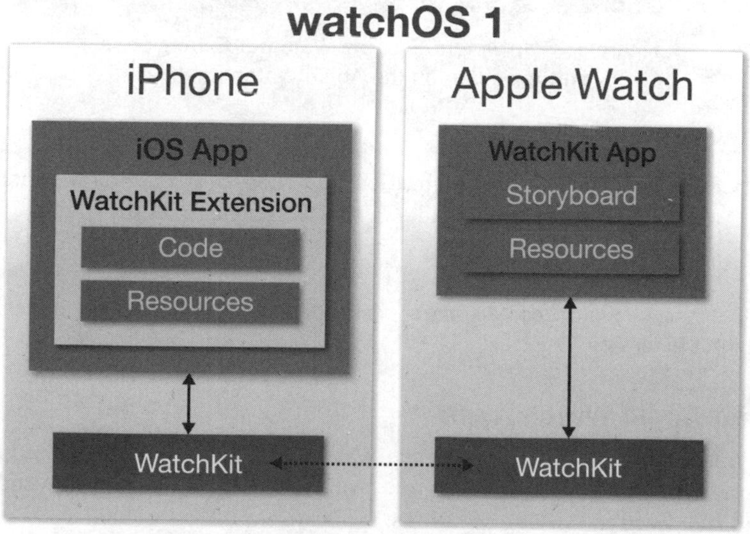

watchOS 1

iPhone	Apple Watch
iOS App	WatchKit App
WatchKit Extension	Storyboard
Code	Resources
Resources	
WatchKit	WatchKit

Figure 1.2   In watchOS 1, the WatchKit Extension is executed by the iPhone

In watchOS 2, the WatchKit Extension is moved to the Apple Watch (see Figure 1.3), so now the UI and application logic of your watch app are executed directly on the watch itself. This model enables developers to build more responsive apps, without having to send data back and forth between the containing iOS app and the watch app. In addition, the watch can connect directly to known WiFi networks, and your watch app can run independently without the help of the paired iPhone.

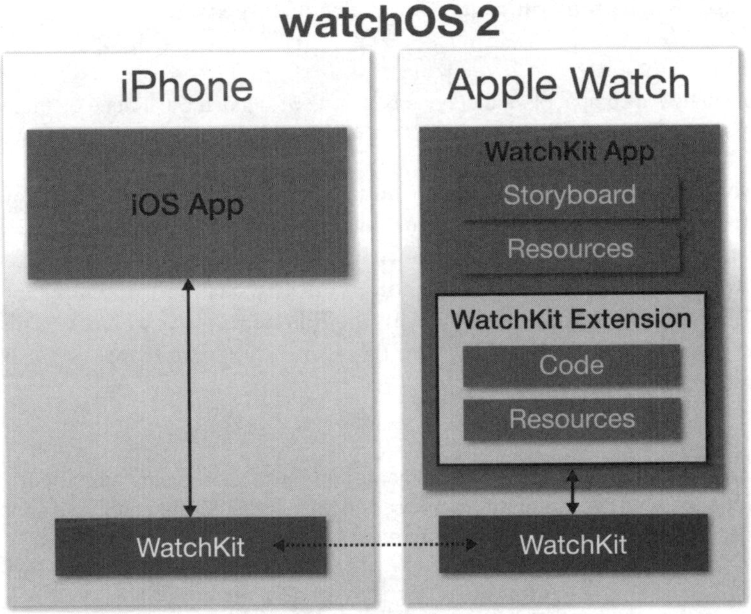

Figure 1.3   In watchOS 2, the WatchKit Extension is now executed on the Apple Watch itself

The WatchKit app only contains the storyboards and resources needed to create the user interface of your Apple Watch application; the code for managing the interactions with your Apple Watch application resides in the WatchKit Extension.

> **Note**
> The WatchKit app does not contain any source code files. All source code files reside in the WatchKit Extension.

Deploying Apple Watch Apps

For deployment, the WatchKit app and the WatchKit Extension are packaged together within a single iOS app bundle (see Figure 1.4). So, to develop an Apple Watch application, you first need to develop an iPhone application.

iOS App Bundle

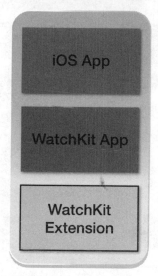

Figure 1.4   The WatchKit Extension and the WatchKit app
must be bundled within an iOS app bundle

When the user installs an iOS application containing the WatchKit app and WatchKit Extension, he or she is prompted to install the WatchKit app and extension if a paired Apple Watch is available. Once the WatchKit app and Extension are installed on the Apple Watch, the watch app can be launched directly from the Apple Watch Home screen.

Interaction between the Apple Watch and iPhone

There are times when your watch application needs to communicate with the containing iOS application. For example, the iPhone may be tracking the location of the user and trying to find a nearby restaurant. When a restaurant is found, the iPhone app would like to send the restaurant details to the Apple Watch. On the Apple Watch, the watch application might also need to communicate with the iPhone app, such as if the user wants to save the particular restaurant to his or her Favorites list on the iPhone.

To facilitate communications between the iPhone app and the watch app, Apple provides the *Watch Connectivity Framework*. Figure 1.5 shows the Watch Connectivity Framework providing a communication link between the watch app and its corresponding iOS app.

Note

Chapter 7, "Interfacing with iOS Apps," discusses the Watch Connectivity Framework in detail.

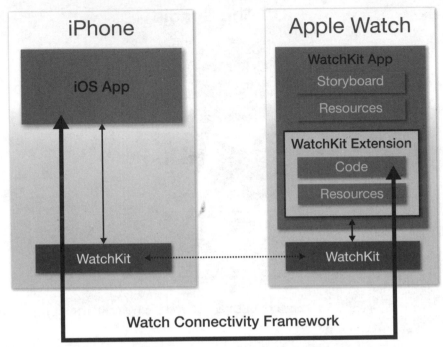

Figure 1.5   Interactions with the Watch app and the iOS app are
handled by the Watch Connectivity Framework

Types of Apple Watch Applications

For this release of the WatchKit framework, you can develop the following types of
Apple Watch applications:

- **WatchKit apps**: Apps that run on the Apple Watch and interact with the containing iOS app on the iPhone.
- **Glances**: A supplemental way for the user to view important information from your app. Glances do not support interactions with users—tapping on a glance launches the WatchKit app. Chapter 9, "Displaying Glances," discusses glances in more detail.
- **Notifications**: Displays notifications received by the iPhone (either local or remote notifications); apps can customize the notification interface. (Chapter 8, "Displaying Notifications," discusses notifications.)
- **Complications**: Complications are display elements on watch faces that display data from applications like Activity, Calendar, Weather, and so on. In this version of WatchKit, your application can display complications data on watch faces. (Chapter 6, "Programming Complications," discusses complications.)

Hello, World!

Now that we have all the basics covered, you must be raring to go and yearning to get your hands dirty! So, without further ado, make sure you download and install Xcode and let's create your first Apple Watch app!

Creating an iPhone Project

The first step toward creating an Apple Watch application is to create an iPhone application. To do this, follow these steps:

1. Launch Xcode and select the **iOS App with WatchKit App** template (see Figure 1.6).

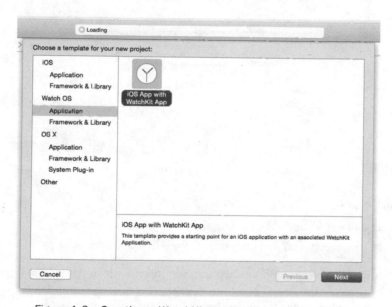

Figure 1.6 Creating a WatchKit application project in Xcode

2. Click **Next**.
3. Name the project as follows (see Figure 1.7):

   Product Name: HelloAppleWatch.

   Organization Name: Either your name or your organization's name.

   Organization Identifier: Usually, the reverse domain name of your organization (e.g., *com.example*). The Bundle Identifier is formed by concatenating the Organization Name with the Product Name. If you intend to host your app on the App Store, the Bundle Identifier of your app must be unique.

Language: Swift.

Devices: iPhone.

Ensure that all the other options are unchecked.

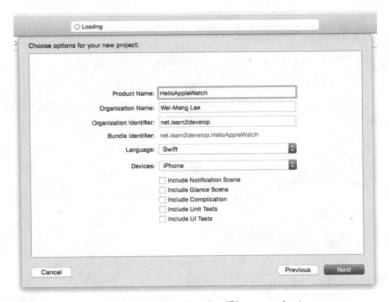

Figure 1.7   Naming the iPhone project

4. Click **Next**.

5. Select a folder on your Mac to save the project, and click **Create**.

    When the project is created successfully, you will see Xcode, as shown in Figure 1.8.

What you now have is an iPhone application project with an embedded WatchKit application. Observe the targets you have in your project, as shown in Figure 1.9.

In particular, observe the three highlighted groups:

- **HelloAppleWatch**: The iOS app that acts as the container for the watch application
- **HelloAppleWatch WatchKit App**: The WatchKit app that contains the UI of your watch application
- **HelloAppleWatch WatchKit Extension**: The WatchKit Extension that contains the application logic of your watch application

Observe that the HelloAppleWatch WatchKit App target contains the Interface .storyboard file. This is the storyboard file that contains the UI of your watch application. The HelloAppleWatch WatchKit Extension target, on the other hand, contains the InterfaceController.swift and ExtensionDelegate.swift files, which is the code that is executed when the user interacts with the watch application.

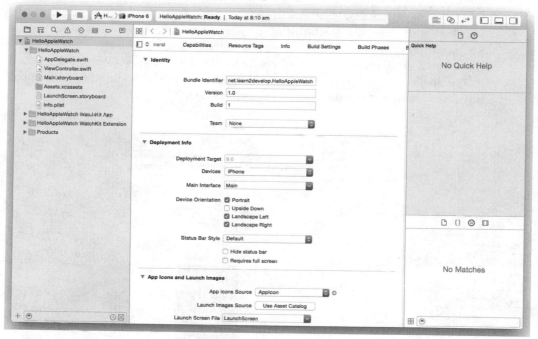

Figure 1.8   The project created in Xcode

Figure 1.9   The three main components of the project: the containing
iOS app, the WatchKit app, and the WatchKit Extension

Examining the Storyboard

Let's look at the Interface.storyboard file located in the HelloAppleWatch WatchKit App target. Selecting the file displays it using the Storyboard Editor (see Figure 1.10). It contains a single Interface Controller, which is similar to a View Controller in your iPhone application. When the user loads the application on the Apple Watch, the initial Interface Controller from the main storyboard is loaded.

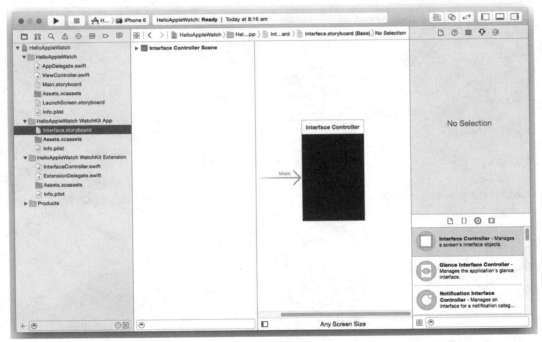

Figure 1.10   The Interface Controller representing the UI of your Apple Watch app

When you select the Interface Controller and examine the Class attribute under the Identity Inspector window, you will see that it is connected to a class known as `InterfaceController` (see Figure 1.11).

WatchKit App Lifecycle

The `InterfaceController` class is stored in the file named InterfaceController.swift. It is located within the HelloAppleWatch WatchKit Extension target. Listing 1.1 shows the content of the `InterfaceController` class.

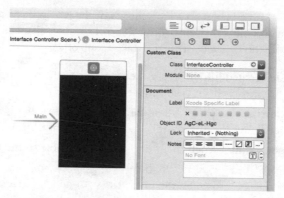

Figure 1.11   The class representing the Interface Controller

Listing 1.1   **Content of the `InterfaceController` Class**

```
import WatchKit
import Foundation


class InterfaceController: WKInterfaceController {

    override func awakeWithContext(context: AnyObject?) {
        super.awakeWithContext(context)

        // Configure interface objects here.
    }

    override func willActivate() {
        // This method is called when watch view controller is
        // about to be visible to user.
        super.willActivate()
    }

    override func didDeactivate() {
        // This method is called when watch view controller is
        // no longer visible.
        super.didDeactivate()
    }

}
```

The `InterfaceController` class is a subclass of the `WKInterfaceController` class. When subclassing the `WKInterfaceController` class, you can override a couple of methods to handle the lifecycle of an Interface Controller:

- **init**—The designated initializer for the Interface Controller objects. Note that Xcode does not create this method by default.
- **awakeWithContext:**—Fired when the Interface Controller is displayed for the first time; useful for object initializations, updating your UI, etc.
- **willActivate**—Fired when the user interface is visible to the user; useful for updating the user interface, setting up timers, etc.
- **didDeactivate**—Fired when the user exits your app explicitly or stops interacting with the Apple Watch; useful for cleaning up resources, saving data, etc.

> **Note**
>
> Chapter 2, "Apple Watch Interface Navigation," discusses the lifecycles of the Interface Controller in detail.

In addition to the InterfaceController.swift file, the WatchKit Extension target also includes the ExtensionDelegate.swift file. Its use is very similar to that of the AppDelegate.swift file in the iOS app—it handles events that are fired when your watch application has finished launching, becomes active, or becomes inactive. Listing 1.2 shows the content of the `ExtensionDelegate` class.

Listing 1.2   Content of the `ExtensionDelegate` Class

```
import WatchKit

class ExtensionDelegate: NSObject, WKExtensionDelegate {

    func applicationDidFinishLaunching() {
        // Perform any final initialization of your application.
    }

    func applicationDidBecomeActive() {
        // Restart any tasks that were paused (or not yet started) while the
        // application was inactive. If the application was previously in
        // the background, optionally refresh the user interface.
    }

    func applicationWillResignActive() {
        // Sent when the application is about to move from active to
        // inactive state. This can occur for certain types of temporary
        // interruptions (such as an incoming phone call or SMS message) or
```

```
    // when the user quits the application and it begins the transition to
    // the background state.
    // Use this method to pause ongoing tasks, disable timers, etc.
  }

}
```

Modifying the Interface Controller

Now that we have discussed the underlying details of the parts that make everything work, it is time to do something visual and fun! In the Interface Controller found inside the Interface.storyboard file, drag and drop a Label control (from the Object Library) onto it (see Figure 1.12).

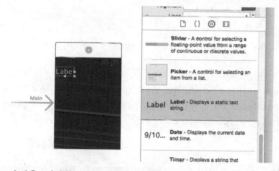

Figure 1.12   Adding a Label control to the Interface Controller

Double-click the Label control and type **Hello, World!**, as shown in Figure 1.13.

Figure 1.13   Typing some text into the Label control

Running the Application on the Simulator

Finally, you are ready to test the application on the iPhone and Apple Watch Simulators. In Xcode, you need to first set the scheme to **HelloAppleWatch WatckKit App** (see Figure 1.14). Also, ensure that **iPhone 6 + Apple Watch – 38mm** is selected. Once this is done, press Command-R to deploy the application onto the iPhone Simulator.

Figure 1.14   Ensure that the HelloAppleWatch WatchKit App scheme is selected before running the project

> **Note**
>
> You can choose to test your application on either the 38mm or 42mm Apple Watch Simulator.

The first time you launch the iPhone and Apple Watch Simulators, you may see a prompt on the iPhone Simulator, requesting permission for the Apple Watch Faces to access your location. Click **Allow** (see Figure 1.15).

Figure 1.15   The iPhone Simulator asking for permission to allow the Apple Watch Faces to access your current location

You should now see the Apple Watch Simulator running the application (see Figure 1.16).

Figure 1.16   Your first Apple Watch application running on the Apple Watch Simulator

Note that only the watch app runs on the Apple Watch Simulator; the iOS app is installed on the iPhone Simulator, but it's not launched.

Summary

In this chapter, you learned the basics of developing for the Apple Watch. You first read about the specifications of the watch, and then you learned about the architecture of third-party apps that you can build. Most importantly, in watchOS 2, the processing of your Apple Watch app is now performed on the Apple Watch, rather than on the iPhone as in watchOS 1. This change is significant because you can now write responsive watch apps that run natively on the Apple Watch. It also allows you to access the hardware features of the watch, such as the accelerometer.

You also wrote your first Apple Watch application and tested it on the Apple Watch Simulator. In the next few chapters, you learn more about the different views that you can use to build the UI of your Apple Watch applications, as well as topics such as how to communicate between the containing iOS app and the Apple Watch app.

Apple Watch Interface Navigation

It's really hard to design products by focus groups. A lot of times,
people don't know what they want until you show it to them.

Steve Jobs

In Chapter 1, "Getting Started with WatchKit Programming," you learned about the various specifications and features of the Apple Watch. You also had the chance to use Xcode to create a simple iPhone project that supports the Apple Watch. You then used the Apple Watch Simulator to test the application. In this chapter, you dive into how your Apple Watch application navigates between multiple screens.

Interface Controllers and Storyboard

As you learned in Chapter 1, the user interface of your Apple Watch application is encapsulated in a storyboard file. Within the storyboard file, you have an Interface Controller that represents a screen on the Apple Watch. In this section, let's create a project so that we can examine the storyboard in more detail:

1. Using Xcode, create an iOS App with WatchKit App project and name it **LifeCycle**. Uncheck the option Include Notification Scene so that we can keep the WatchKit project to a bare minimum.

2. Select the Interface.storyboard file located within the LifeCycle WatchKit App group (see Figure 2.1). This opens the file using the Storyboard Editor.

3. Select the Interface Controller and view its Identity Inspector window (see Figure 2.2). The Class is set to `InterfaceController`, which means that it is represented by a Swift class named `InterfaceController`.

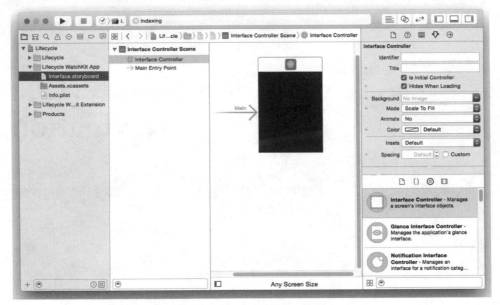

Figure 2.1   Editing the storyboard file

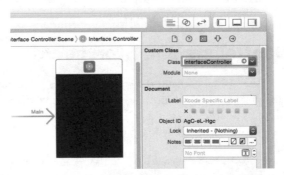

Figure 2.2   The Interface Controller is represented by a
Swift class named `InterfaceController`

4. View its Attributes Inspector window and observe that the Is Initial Controller
   attribute is checked (see Figure 2.3). This attribute indicates that, when the application is loaded, this is the default Interface Controller that will be displayed.

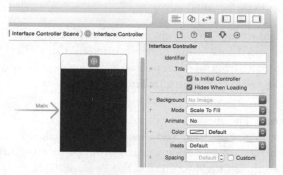

Figure 2.3 The Is Initial Controller attribute indicates that the current InterfaceController will be displayed when the application loads

Lifecycle of an Interface Controller

As you have seen in the previous section and in Chapter 1, an Interface Controller is connected to a Swift class located in the WatchKit Extension group of the project. In this example, this Swift class is named InterfaceController.swift. It has the following content:

```
import WatchKit
import Foundation

class InterfaceController: WKInterfaceController {

    override func awakeWithContext(context: AnyObject?) {
        super.awakeWithContext(context)

        // Configure interface objects here.
    }

    override func willActivate() {
        // This method is called when watch view controller is about
        // to be visible to user
        super.willActivate()
    }

    override func didDeactivate() {
        // This method is called when watch view controller is no
        // longer visible
        super.didDeactivate()
    }

}
```

Specifically, it has three key methods:

- **awakeWithContext:**—The system calls this method at initialization time, passing it any contextual data from a previous Interface Controller. You should use this method to initialize and to prepare your UI for display, as well as to obtain any data that is passed to it from another Interface Controller (you will learn how this is done in the later section on passing data).

- **willActivate**—This method is called by the system when the Interface Controller is about to be displayed. You should use this method to make some last-minute changes to your UI and refrain from performing any tasks that initialize the UI—these should be done in the awakeWithContext method.

- **didDeactivate**—This method is called when the Interface Controller is no longer onscreen. You should use this method to perform cleanup operations on your Interface Controller, such as invalidating timers or saving state-related information.

Besides the three methods just discussed, you can also add an initializer to the Interface Controller class:

```
override init() {
    super.init()
}
```

You can also perform initialization for your Interface Controller in this initializer, but you should leave the bulk of the UI initialization to the awakeWithContext: method. Let's try an example to better understand the use of the various methods:

1. Add the following statements in bold to the InterfaceController.swift file:

```
import WatchKit
import Foundation

class InterfaceController: WKInterfaceController {

    override init() {
        super.init()
        print("In the init initializer")
    }

    override func awakeWithContext(context: AnyObject?) {
        super.awakeWithContext(context)

        // Configure interface objects here.
        print("In the awakeWithContext event")
    }
```

```
override func willActivate() {
    // This method is called when watch view controller is about
    // to be visible to user
    super.willActivate()
    print("In the willActivate event")
}

override func didDeactivate() {
    // This method is called when watch view controller is no
    // longer visible
    super.didDeactivate()
    print("In the didDeactivate event")
}

}
```

2. Select the WatchKit app scheme and run the application on the Apple Watch
   Simulator. When the application is loaded onto the Apple Watch Simulator, you
   should see the statements printed out in the Output window in Xcode, as shown
   in Figure 2.4. Observe that the init, awakeWithContext:, and willActivate
   methods are fired when the Interface Controller is loaded.

   > **Note**
   >
   > If you are not able to see the Output window, press Command-Shift-C in Xcode.

Figure 2.4   Examining the events that are fired
when an Interface Controller is loaded

3. With the Apple Watch Simulator selected, select **Hardware | Lock** to lock
   the Apple Watch. Observe the output in the Output window (see Figure 2.5).
   Observe that the didDeactivate method is now executed.

> **Note**
>
> The `didDeactivate` method is also fired when an Interface Controller transits to another Interface Controller.

Figure 2.5   Examining the event that is fired when an
Interface Controller is deactivated

> **Note**
>
> To unlock the Apple Watch Simulator, unlock the iPhone Simulator by selecting **Hardware | Home**.

Navigating between Interface Controllers

The basic unit of display for an Apple Watch app is represented by an Interface Controller (of type `WKInterfaceController`). Depending on the type of application you are working on, there are times when you need to spread your UI across multiple Interface Controllers. In Apple Watch, there are two ways to navigate between Interface Controllers:

- **Hierarchical**: Pushes another Interface Controller on the screen. This model is usually used when you want the user to follow a series of related steps in order to perform a particular action.
- **Page-Based**: Displays another Interface Controller on top of the current Interface Controller. This model is usually used if the information displayed on each Interface Controller is not closely related to other Interface Controllers. You can also use this model to display a series of Interface Controllers, which the user can select by swiping the screen.

> **Similarities to iPhone Development**
>
> The page-based navigation method is similar to presenting a modal View Controller in iPhone, whereas the hierarchical navigation method is similar to using a navigation controller in iPhone.

Hierarchical Navigation

A hierarchical interface always starts with a root Interface Controller. It then pushes additional Interface Controllers when a button or a control in a screen is tapped.

1. Using Xcode, create an iOS App with WatchKit App project and name it **UINavigations**. Uncheck the option Include Notification Scene so that we can keep the WatchKit project to a bare minimum.

2. In the UINavigation WatchKit App group, select the Interface.storyboard file to edit it in the Storyboard Editor.

3. Drag and drop another Interface Controller object onto the editor, as shown in Figure 2.6. You should now have two Interface Controllers.

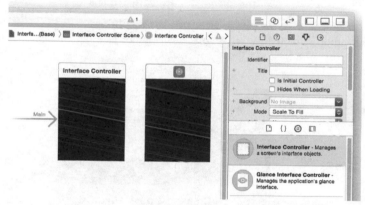

Figure 2.6   Adding another Interface Controller to the storyboard

4. In the original Interface Controller, add a Button control (see Figure 2.7) and change its title (by double-clicking it) to **Next Screen**.

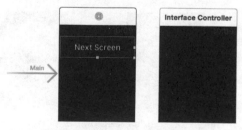

Figure 2.7   Adding a Button control to the first Interface Controller

5. Control–click the **Next Screen** button and drag it over the second Interface Controller (see Figure 2.8).

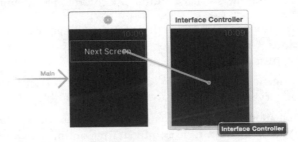

Figure 2.8 Control-click the Button control and drag it over the second Interface Controller

6. You see a popup called Action Segue. Select **push** (see Figure 2.9).

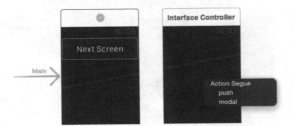

Figure 2.9 Creating a push segue

A segue has been created (see Figure 2.10), linking the first Interface Controller to the second.

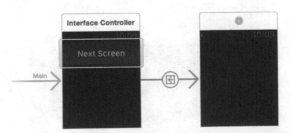

Figure 2.10 The segue that is created after performing the action

7. Select the segue and set its Identifier to **hierarchical** in the Attributes Inspector window (see Figure 2.11). This identifier allows us to identify it programmatically in our code later.

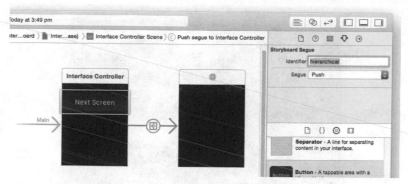

Figure 2.11   Naming the Identifier for the segue

8. Add a Label control to the second Interface Controller, as shown in Figure 2.12. Set the Lines attribute of the Label control to **0** in the Attributes Inspector window so that the label can wrap around long text (used later in this chapter).

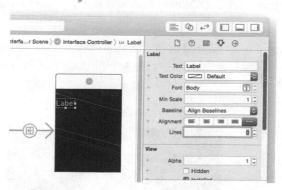

Figure 2.12   Adding a Label control to the second Interface Controller

9. You are now ready to test the application. Select the WatchKit app scheme and run the application on the Apple Watch Simulator. Click the **Next Screen** button and observe that the application navigates to the second Interface Controller containing the Label control (see Figure 2.13). Also, observe that the second Interface Controller has a < icon (known as a *chevron*) displayed in the top-left corner. Clicking it returns the application to the first Interface Controller.

Note

At this point, the Label control on the second Interface Controller is still displaying the default text "Label." In later sections in this chapter, you learn how to pass data from the first Interface Controller to the second and then how to display the data in the Label control.

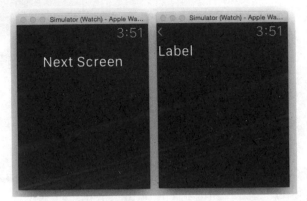

Figure 2.13   Navigating to another Interface
Controller using hierarchical navigation

Page-Based Navigation

You can also display an Interface Controller modally. This is useful if you want to obtain some information from the user or get the user to confirm an action.

1. Using the same project created in the previous section, add another Button control to the first Interface Controller, as shown in Figure 2.14. Change the title of the button to **Display Screen**.

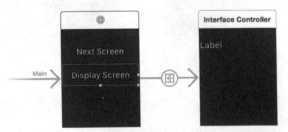

Figure 2.14   Adding another Button control to
the first Interface Controller

2. Create a segue connecting the **Display Screen** button to the second Interface Controller. In the popup that appears, select **modal**. Set the Identifier of the newly created segue to **pagebased** (see Figure 2.15).

3. Select the WatchKit app scheme and run the application on the Apple Watch Simulator. Click the **Display Screen** button and observe that the second Interface Controller appears from the bottom of the screen. Also, observe that the second Interface Controller now has a **Cancel** button displayed in the top-left corner (see Figure 2.16). Clicking it hides the second Interface Controller.

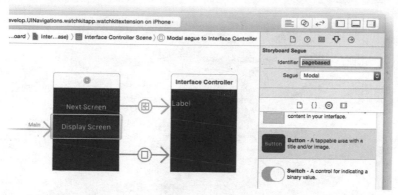

Figure 2.15   Creating a modal segue connecting the two Interface Controllers

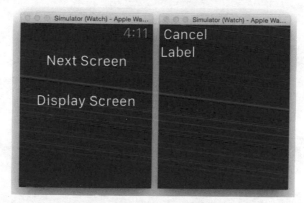

Figure 2.16   Displaying another Interface Controller modally

Passing Data between Interface Controllers

In the previous sections, you saw how to make your Apple Watch application transit from one Interface Controller to another, using either the hierarchical or page-based navigation method. One commonly performed task is to pass data from one Interface Controller to another. In this section, you do just that.

1. Using the UINavigation project that you used in the previous section, right-click the **UINavigation WatchKit Extension** and select **New File…** (see Figure 2.17).

2. Select the **WatchKit Class** (see Figure 2.18) template and click **Next**.

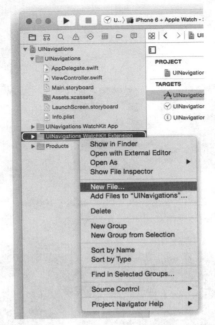

Figure 2.17   Adding a new file to the project

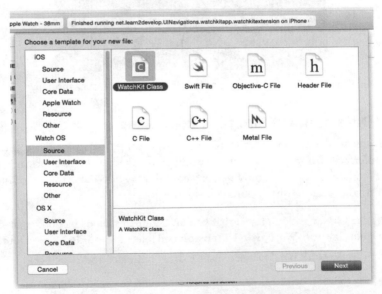

Figure 2.18   Selecting the WatchKit Class template

3. Name the Class `SecondInterfaceController` and make it a subclass of `WKInterfaceController` (see Figure 2.19). Click **Next**.

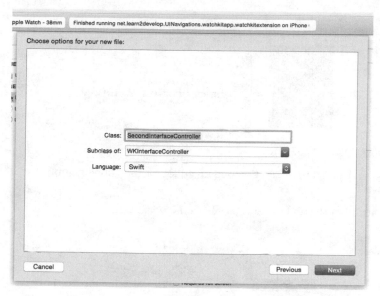

Figure 2.19   Naming the newly added class

4. A file named SecondInterfaceController.swift is now added to the UINavigation
   WatchKit Extension.

5. Back in the Storyboard Editor, select the second Interface Controller and set its
   Class (in the Identity Inspector window) to SecondInterfaceController
   (see Figure 2.20).

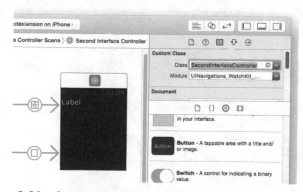

Figure 2.20   Setting the class of the second Interface Controller

6. Select the **View | Assistant Editor | Show Assistant Editor** menu item to
   show the Assistant Editor. Control-click the Label control and drag it onto the
   Code Editor (as shown in Figure 2.21).

Figure 2.21   Creating an outlet for the Label control

7. Create an outlet and name it **label** (see Figure 2.22).

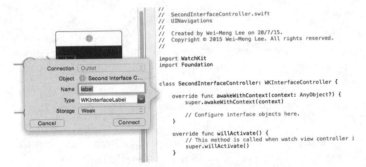

Figure 2.22   Naming the outlet for the Label control

An outlet is now added to the code:

```
import WatchKit
import Foundation

class SecondInterfaceController: WKInterfaceController {

    @IBOutlet var label: WKInterfaceLabel!

    override func awakeWithContext(context: AnyObject?) {
        super.awakeWithContext(context)

        // Configure interface objects here.
    }
```

8. Add the following statements in bold to the InterfaceController.swift file:

```
import WatchKit
import Foundation
```

```
class InterfaceController: WKInterfaceController {

    override func awakeWithContext(context: AnyObject?) {
        super.awakeWithContext(context)

        // Configure interface objects here.
    }

    override func willActivate() {
        // This method is called when watch view controller is about
        // to be visible to user
        super.willActivate()
    }

    override func didDeactivate() {
        // This method is called when watch view controller is
        // no longer visible
        super.didDeactivate()
    }

    override func contextForSegueWithIdentifier(segueIdentifier: String) ->
    AnyObject? {
        switch segueIdentifier {
            case "hierarchical":return [
                "segue": "hierarchical",
                "data" : "Passed through hierarchical navigation"
                ]
            case "pagebased":return [
                "segue": "pagebased",
                "data" : "Passed through page-based navigation"
                ]
            default:return [
                "segue": "",
                "data" : ""
                ]
        }
    }
}
```

The contextForSegueWithIdentifier: method is fired before any of the
segues fire (when the user taps on one of the Button controls). Here, you check
the identifier of the segue (through the segueIdentifier argument). Specifically, you return a dictionary containing two keys: segue and data. The data
you returned here will be passed to the target Interface Controller.

9. Add the following statements in bold to the SecondInterfaceController.swift file:

```
import WatchKit
import Foundation
```

```
class SecondInterfaceController: WKInterfaceController {

    @IBOutlet var label: WKInterfaceLabel!
    override func awakeWithContext(context: AnyObject?) {
        super.awakeWithContext(context)

        // Configure interface objects here.
        if let dict = context as? [String : String] {
            let segue = dict["segue"]
            let data = dict["data"]
            self.label.setText(segue! + " - " + data!)
        }

    }
}
```

When the second Interface Controller is loaded, you retrieve the data that is passed into it in the awakeWithContext: method through the context argument. Because the first Interface Controller passes in a dictionary, you can typecast it into a dictionary object and then retrieve the value of the segue and data keys. The value of the data key is then displayed in the Label control.

10. Select the WatchKit app scheme and run the application on the Apple Watch Simulator. Click the **Next Screen** button, and observe the string displayed in the second Interface Controller (see Figure 2.23).

Figure 2.23   Displaying the data passed through
the hierarchical navigation

11. Click the < chevron to return to the first Interface Controller and click the **Display Screen** button. Observe the string displayed in the second Interface Controller (see Figure 2.24).

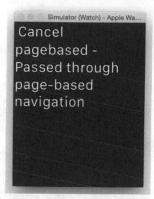

Figure 2.24   Displaying the data passed
through page-based navigation

Customizing the Title of the Chevron or Cancel Button

As you have seen in the previous section, a chevron is displayed when you push an Interface Controller using the hierarchical navigation method. A default **Cancel** button is displayed when you display an Interface Controller modally. However, the chevron or **Cancel** button can be customized.

1. Add the following statements in bold to the SecondInterfaceController.swift file:

```
import WatchKit
import Foundation

class SecondInterfaceController: WKInterfaceController {

    @IBOutlet var label: WKInterfaceLabel!
    override func awakeWithContext(context: AnyObject?) {
        super.awakeWithContext(context)

        // Configure interface objects here.
        if let dict = context as? [String : String] {
            let segue = dict["segue"]
            let data = dict["data"]
            self.label.setText(segue! + " - " + data!)

            if segue == "pagebased" {
                self.setTitle("Close")
            } else {
                self.setTitle("Back")
            }
        }
    }
}
```

2. Select the WatchKit app scheme and run the application on the Apple Watch Simulator. Click the **Next Screen** button, and observe the string displayed next to the chevron (see Figure 2.25).

Figure 2.25   Displaying a string next to the chevron

3. Click the **<Back** chevron to return to the first Interface Controller and click the **Display Screen** button. Observe that the **Cancel** button is now displayed as **Close** (see Figure 2.26).

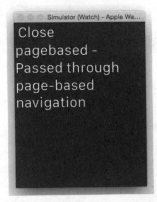

Figure 2.26   Modifying the button for a modal Interface Controller

Navigating Using Code

Although you can link up Interface Controllers by creating segues in your storyboard, it is not versatile. In a real-life application, the flow of your application may depend on certain conditions being met, and hence, you need to be able to decide during runtime which Interface Controller to navigate to (or display modally).

1. Using Xcode, create a new iOS App with WatchKit App project and name it **NavigateUsingCode**. Uncheck the option Include Notification Scene so that we can keep the WatchKit project to a bare minimum.

2. Click the Interface.storyboard file located in the NavigateUsingCode WatchKit App group in your project to edit it using the Storyboard Editor.

3. Add two Button controls to the first Interface Controller and then add another Interface Controller to the storyboard. In the second Interface Controller, add a Label control, as shown in Figure 2.27.

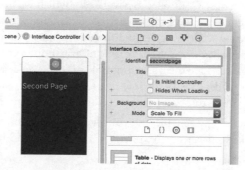

Figure 2.27   Populating the two Interface Controllers

4. Select the second Interface Controller and set its Identifier attribute (in the Attributes Inspector window) to **secondpage**, as shown in Figure 2.28.

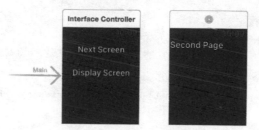

Figure 2.28   Setting the Identifier attribute
for the second Interface Controller

5. In the first Interface Controller, create two actions (one for each button) and name them as shown below in the InterfaceController.swift file. You should create the actions by control-dragging them from the storyboard onto the Code Editor.

```
import WatchKit
import Foundation
```

```
class InterfaceController: WKInterfaceController {

    @IBAction func btnNextScreen() {
    }

    @IBAction func btnDisplayScreen() {
    }
```

6. Add the following statements to the two actions in the InterfaceController.swift file:

```
import WatchKit
import Foundation

class InterfaceController: WKInterfaceController {

    @IBAction func btnNextScreen() {
        pushControllerWithName("secondpage", context: nil)
    }

    @IBAction func btnDisplayScreen() {
        presentControllerWithName("secondpage", context: nil)
    }
```

Observe that the first button uses the pushControllerWithName:context: method to perform a hierarchical navigation. The first argument to this method takes in the identifier of the Interface Controller to navigate to (which we had earlier set in Step 4). The context argument allows you to pass data to the target Interface Controller (discussed in the previous section), which in this case we simply set to nil. For the second button, we use the presentControllerWithName:context: method to perform page-based navigation. Like the pushControllerWithName:context: method, the first argument is the identifier of the Interface Controller to display, whereas the second argument allows you to pass data to the target Interface Controller.

7. Select the WatchKit app scheme and run the application on the Apple Watch Simulator. Clicking either button brings you to the second Interface Controller (see Figure 2.29).

> ### Returning to the Previous Screen
>
> Although you can return to the previous screen by tapping either the chevron or the **Cancel** button, you can also programmatically return to the previous screen. If you navigate to an Interface Controller using the pushControllerWithName:context: method, you can programmatically return to the Interface Controller using the corresponding popController method. If you display an Interface Controller using the presentControllerWithName:context: method, you can dismiss the current Interface Controller using the corresponding dismissController method.

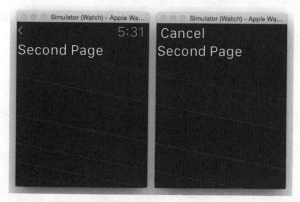

Figure 2.29   Navigating the Interface Controllers programmatically

Presenting a Series of Pages

For page-based applications, you can display more than one single Interface Controller modally—you can display a series of them:

1. Using the same project created in the previous section, add a third Interface Controller to the storyboard and add a Label control to it. Set the label text to **Third Page** (see Figure 2.30).

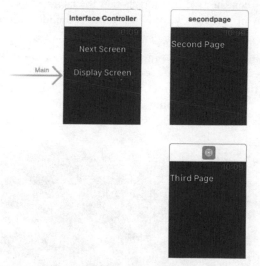

Figure 2.30   Adding the third Interface Controller

2. Set the Identifier attribute of the third Interface Controller to **thirdpage** in the Attributes Inspector window (see Figure 2.31).

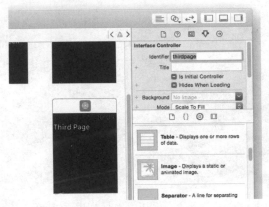

Figure 2.31   Setting the Identifier for the third Interface Controller

3. Add the following statements in bold to the InterfaceController.swift file:

```
@IBAction func btnDisplayScreen() {
    // presentControllerWithName("secondpage", context: nil)
    presentControllerWithNames(["secondpage", "thirdpage"], contexts: nil)
}
```

Instead of using the `presentControllerWithName:context:` method, we now use the `presentControllerWithNames:context:` method. The only difference between the two methods is that the latter takes in an array of string in the first argument. This array of string contains the identifiers of Interface Controllers that you want to display.

4. Select the WatchKit app scheme and run the application on the Apple Watch Simulator. Click the **Display Screen** button on the Apple Watch Simulator. This time, you see that the second Interface Controller is displayed with two dots at the bottom of the screen. Swiping from right to left reveals the third Interface Controller (see Figure 2.32).

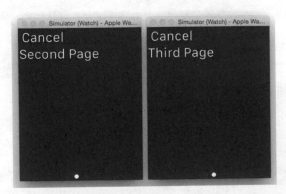

Figure 2.32   The user can slide between the two Interface Controllers

Changing the Current Page to Display

In the previous section, you saw that you could display a series of Interface Controllers that the user can swipe through. What if you want to programmatically jump to a particular page? In this case, what if you want to display the Third Page instead of the Second Page? Let's see how this can be done:

1. Add two WatchKit Class files (make them subclasses of WKInterfaceController) to the WatchKit Extension and name them **SecondInterfaceController.swift** and **ThirdInterfaceController.swift**, respectively. Figure 2.33 shows the location of the files.

Figure 2.33   Adding the two Swift files to the project

2. Populate the SecondInterfaceController.swift file as follows:

```swift
import WatchKit
import Foundation

class SecondInterfaceController: WKInterfaceController {

    override func awakeWithContext(context: AnyObject?) {
        super.awakeWithContext(context)

        // Configure interface objects here.
        print("SecondInterfaceController - awakeWithContext")
    }

    override func willActivate() {
        // This method is called when watch view controller is about
        // to be visible to user.
        super.willActivate()
        print("SecondInterfaceController - willActivate")
    }
```

```
      override func didDeactivate() {
          // This method is called when watch view controller is
          // no longer visible.
          super.didDeactivate()
          print("SecondInterfaceController - didDeactivate")
      }


  }
```

3. Populate the ThirdInterfaceController.swift file as follows:

```
import WatchKit
import Foundation

class ThirdInterfaceController: WKInterfaceController {

      override func awakeWithContext(context: AnyObject?) {
          super.awakeWithContext(context)

          // Configure interface objects here.
          print("ThirdInterfaceController - awakeWithContext")
      }

      override func willActivate() {
          // This method is called when watch view controller is about
          // to be visible to user
          super.willActivate()
          print("ThirdInterfaceController - willActivate")
      }

      override func didDeactivate() {
          // This method is called when watch view controller is
          // no longer visible
          super.didDeactivate()
          print("ThirdInterfaceController - didDeactivate")
      }

  }
```

4. In the Interface.storyboard file, set the Class property of the second Interface Controller to **SecondInterfaceController** (see Figure 2.34). Likewise, set the Class property of the third Interface Controller to **ThirdInterfaceController**.

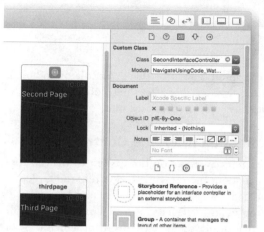

Figure 2.34 Setting the class for the second Interface Controller

5. Select the WatchKit app scheme and run the application on the Apple Watch Simulator. Click the **Display Screen** button on the Apple Watch Simulator. Observe the statements printed in the Output window (see Figure 2.35). As you can see, the `awakeWithContext:` method is fired for both the second and third Interface Controllers, even though only the second Interface Controller is visible initially.

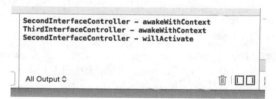

```
SecondInterfaceController - awakeWithContext
ThirdInterfaceController - awakeWithContext
SecondInterfaceController - willActivate


All Output ◇
```

Figure 2.35 Both Interface Controllers fire the `awakeWithContext:` method

6. If you want the third Interface Controller to load instead of the second, you can use the `becomeCurrentPage` method. Calling this method in an Interface Controller brings it into view. Because both the second and third Interface Controllers fire the `awakeWithContext:` method when you click the **Display Screen** button, you can call the `becomeCurrentPage` method in the `awakeWithContext:` method. Add the following statement in bold to the ThirdInterfaceController .swift file:

```swift
override func awakeWithContext(context: AnyObject?) {
    super.awakeWithContext(context)
```

```
            // Configure interface objects here.
            becomeCurrentPage()
            print("ThirdInterfaceController - awakeWithContext")
    }
```

7. Run the application on the Apple Watch Simulator and click the **Display Screen** button. This time, you see that after the second Interface Controller is displayed, it will automatically scroll to the third one.

Returning Data from an Interface Controller

Earlier in this chapter, you saw that you can easily pass data to another Interface Controller. However, what about the reverse? Very often, the target Interface Controller may need to return data back to the calling Interface Controller. For example, the user may click a button in an Interface Controller and the app will navigate to another Interface Controller that displays a list of items from which to select. Once an item is selected, the app returns it back to the original Interface Controller.

To return data back to the calling Interface Controller, there are two main techniques:

- Use the Delegation design pattern where the target Interface Controller defines a protocol that the calling Interface Controller must implement. Once the target Interface Controller is closed, it calls the method that is implemented in the calling Interface Controller and passes it the data that it needs to return. However, this method is not really feasible in the WatchKit framework as both methods of navigation (programmatically or using the storyboard) do not provide an instance of the target Interface Controller. Instead, you navigate using the identifier of the segue or Interface Controller.

- Use the NSNotificationCenter to send notifications to other parts of the app so that they can be notified of changes. In the WatchKit framework, this is the easiest to implement. (Note, however, that this method is harder to maintain as the project grows.) The calling Interface Controller would need to add an observer to a notification that will be fired by the target Interface Controller. The target Interface Controller would then pass the data through the notification.

In the following example, you learn how to return data from an Interface Controller using NSNotificationCenter:

1. Using Xcode, create a new iOS App with WatchKit App project and name it **ReturningValues**. Uncheck the option Include Notification Scene so that we can keep the WatchKit project to a bare minimum.

2. Click the Interface.storyboard file located in the WatchKit App in your project to edit it using the Storyboard Editor.

3. Add a Button control and a Label control to the first Interface Controller, and then add another Interface Controller to the storyboard. In the second Interface Controller, add a Picker and a Button control, as shown in Figure 2.36.

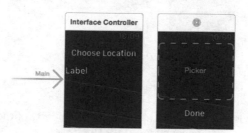

Figure 2.36   Populating the two Interface Controllers

When the user clicks the **Choose Location** button, the app displays the second Interface Controller so that the user can select a location from the Picker control. Clicking the **Done** button will bring the user back to the first Interface Controller, where the location selected will be displayed in the Label control.

4. Set the Identifier attribute of the second Interface Controller to **secondpage** (see Figure 2.37).

Figure 2.37   Setting the Identifier attribute
of the second Interface Controller

5. Add a WatchKit Class file (make it a subclass of WKInterfaceController) to the WatchKit Extension and name it **SecondInterfaceController.swift**.

6. In the Interface.storyboard file, set the Class property of the second Interface Controller to **SecondInterfaceController** (see Figure 2.38).

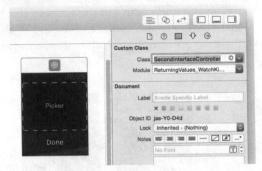

Figure 2.38   Setting the Class property of the
second Interface Controller

7. In the first Interface Controller, create an action for the button and an outlet for
    the Label control and name them as shown below in the InterfaceController.swift
    file. You should create the actions by control-dragging them from the storyboard
    onto the Code Editor.

```
import WatchKit
import Foundation

class InterfaceController: WKInterfaceController {

    @IBOutlet var label: WKInterfaceLabel!

    @IBAction func btnChooseLocation() {
    }
```

8. Add the following statements in bold to the InterfaceController.swift file:

```
import WatchKit
import Foundation

class InterfaceController: WKInterfaceController {

    var location = ""

    @IBOutlet var label: WKInterfaceLabel!

    @IBAction func btnChooseLocation() {
        presentControllerWithName(
            "secondpage",
            context: ["location":location])
    }
```

```swift
override func awakeWithContext(context: AnyObject?) {
    super.awakeWithContext(context)

    // Configure interface objects here.
    NSNotificationCenter.defaultCenter().addObserver(
        self,
        selector: "locationSelected:",
        name: "LOCATION_SELECTED",
        object: nil)
}

//---when a NSNotification is received---
func locationSelected(notification: NSNotification) {
    let data = notification.object as! [String:String]
    location = data["location"]!
}

override func willActivate() {
    // This method is called when watch view controller is about
    // to be visible to user
    super.willActivate()
    label.setText(location)
}

override func didDeactivate() {
    // This method is called when watch view controller is
    // no longer visible
    super.didDeactivate()
}

}
```

When the user clicks the **Choose Location** button, you display the second Interface Controller and pass it a dictionary containing the value of the location variable.

In the awakeWithContext: method, you added a notification observer, with the notification name LOCATION_SELECTED. This is the notification name that will be sent by the second Interface Controller when the user is done selecting a location. Once this notification name is received, it calls the locationSelected: method. The argument of this method has a dictionary with the location key containing the location set as its value. You then update the Label control with this location in the willActivate method.

9. In the second Interface Controller, create two actions (one for the button and one for the Picker) and an outlet for the Picker and name them as shown below in the

SecondInterfaceController.swift file. You should create the actions and outlet by control-dragging them from the storyboard onto the Code Editor.

```swift
import WatchKit
import Foundation

class SecondInterfaceController: WKInterfaceController {

    @IBOutlet var picker: WKInterfacePicker!

    @IBAction func btnPickerSelected(value: Int) {
    }

    @IBAction func btnDone() {
    }
```

10. Add the following statements in bold to the SecondInterfaceController.swift file:

```swift
import WatchKit
import Foundation

class SecondInterfaceController: WKInterfaceController {

    var pickerSelectedIndex = 0
    let locations = [
        "Singapore", "Oslo", "Tokyo", "Denmark", "Copenhagen",
        "Bangkok", "Manila"
    ]

    @IBOutlet var picker: WKInterfacePicker!

    @IBAction func btnPickerSelected(value: Int) {
        //---index of the selected item in the picker---
        pickerSelectedIndex = value
    }

    @IBAction func btnDone() {
        //---post a NSNotification---
        NSNotificationCenter.defaultCenter().postNotificationName(
            "LOCATION_SELECTED",
            object: ["location":locations[pickerSelectedIndex]])

        //---close the current interface controller---
        dismissController()
    }

    override func awakeWithContext(context: AnyObject?) {
        super.awakeWithContext(context)
```

```swift
        // Configure interface objects here.
        var previousLocation = ""
        if let dict = context as? [String : String] {
            previousLocation = dict["location"]!
        }

        //---find the index of the location that should appear
        // selected in the picker--
        if let index = locations.indexOf(previousLocation) {
            pickerSelectedIndex = index
        }

        //---array of WKPickerItem objects---
        var items = [WKPickerItem]()

        for location in locations {
            let item = WKPickerItem()
            item.title = location
            items.append(item)
        }

        //---display all the locations in the picker---
        picker.setItems(items)
    }

override func willActivate() {
        // This method is called when watch view controller is about
        // to be visible to user
        super.willActivate()

        //---display the location previously selected---
        picker.setSelectedItemIndex(pickerSelectedIndex)
    }

override func didDeactivate() {
        // This method is called when watch view controller is
        // no longer visible
        super.didDeactivate()
    }

}
```

In the awakeWithContext: method, you first obtain the location that is passed in. This location represents the location that was previously selected. Its index is in the locations array. Knowing this index allows you to later move the Picker to display the previously selected location.

You then populate the Picker control with an array of `WKPickerItem` objects representing a list of locations. In the `willActivate` method, you make the Picker control display the location that was previously selected. When the user clicks the **Done** button, you post a notification with the name `LOCATION_SELECTED`, together with the name of the location selected.

> **Note**
>
> The Picker control is new in watchOS 2 and will be covered in more detail in Chapter 4, "Displaying and Gathering Information."

11. Select the WatchKit app scheme and run the application on the Apple Watch Simulator. Figure 2.39 shows that when a location is selected in the second Interface Controller, the location name is passed back to the first Interface Controller.

Figure 2.39   The location selected in the Picker control is passed back to the calling Interface Controller

Summary

In this chapter, you delved deeper into how Interface Controllers work in your Apple Watch application. You learned

- The lifecycle of an Interface Controller
- How to navigate between Interface Controllers
- The different methods of displaying an Interface Controller
- How to programmatically display an Interface Controller
- How to display a series of Interface Controllers
- How to pass data between Interface Controllers

Responding to User Actions

If you haven't found it yet, keep looking. Don't settle. As with all matters of the heart, you'll know when you find it. And like any great relationship, it just gets better and better as the years roll on.

Steve Jobs

Designing the user interface (UI) for your Apple Watch application is similar to designing for the iPhone. However, space is at a premium on the Apple Watch, and every millimeter on the screen must be put to good use in order to convey the exact intention of your app.

The UI of an Apple Watch application is represented by various controls (commonly known as *views* in iOS programming), and they are divided into two main categories:

- **Responding to user actions**: Users directly interact with these controls to perform some actions. Examples of such controls are Button, Switch, Slider, Picker, and Table.
- **Displaying information**: These controls mainly display information to the user. Examples of such controls are Label, Image, and Table.

In this and the next chapter, you learn how to use these various controls to build the UI of your application.

Using the Tap Gesture to Interact with Controls

One key way to interact with the Apple Watch is to use the tap gesture. You can tap the following controls:

- Button
- Switch
- Slider
- Table

Let's take a more detailed look at these objects!

> **Note**
>
> I cover the Table control in the next chapter where we discuss controls that display information.

Button

The Button control is the most direct way of interacting with an Apple Watch application. A button can display text as well as a background image. Tapping a button triggers an action on the Interface Controller where you can write the code to perform the appropriate action.

Adding a Button to an Interface Controller

In this section, you create a project that uses a Button control. Subsequent sections show you how to customize the button by creating an action for it and then displaying its title using custom fonts.

1. Using Xcode, create a new iOS App with WatchKit App project and name it **Buttons**. Uncheck the option Include Notification Scene so that we can keep the WatchKit project to a bare minimum.

2. Select the Interface.storyboard file to edit it in the Storyboard Editor.

3. Drag and drop a Button control onto the storyboard, as shown in Figure 3.1.

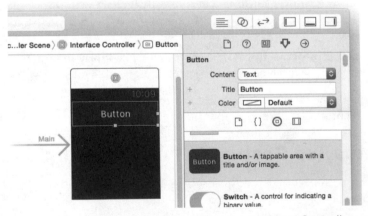

Figure 3.1   Adding a Button control to the Interface Controller

4. In the Attributes Inspector window, set the Title attribute to **Play** (see Figure 3.2).

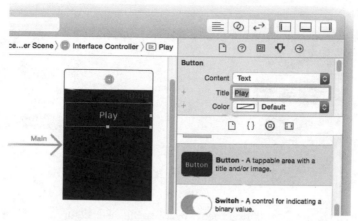

Figure 3.2   Changing the title of the button

5. Select the WatchKit App scheme and run the project on the Apple Watch Simulator. You should see the button on the Apple Watch Simulator (see Figure 3.3). You can click it (or tap it on a real Apple Watch).

Figure 3.3   Testing the button on the Apple Watch Simulator

Creating an Action for a Button

For the Button control to do anything useful, you need to create an action for it so that when the user taps it, your application performs some actions. To create this action, follow these steps:

1. In the Storyboard Editor, select the **View | Assistant Editor | Show Assistant Editor** menu item to show the InterfaceController.swift file.

2. Control-click the Button control in the Interface Controller and drag it over the `InterfaceController` class (see Figure 3.4).

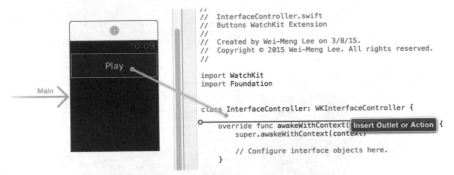

Figure 3.4   Creating an action for the button

3. Create an action for the button and name it **btnPlay** (see Figure 3.5). Click **Connect**.

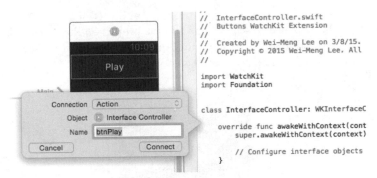

Figure 3.5   Naming the action

4. You now see the action created in the InterfaceController.swift file:

```
import WatchKit
import Foundation

class InterfaceController: WKInterfaceController {

    @IBAction func btnPlay() {
    }
```

5. Add the following statement in bold to the InterfaceController.swift file:

```
@IBAction func btnPlay() {
    print("The button was tapped!")
}
```

6. Select the WatchKit App scheme and run the project on the Apple Watch Simulator. Click the **Play** button and observe the statement printed in the Output window (see Figure 3.6).

Figure 3.6   Clicking the button fires the action

Creating an Outlet for a Button

You can also programmatically change the title of the Button control during runtime. To do so, you need to create an outlet for the button:

1. With the Assistant Editor shown, control-click the button and drag it over the InterfaceController.swift file. Name the outlet **button1** (see Figure 3.7) and click **Connect**.

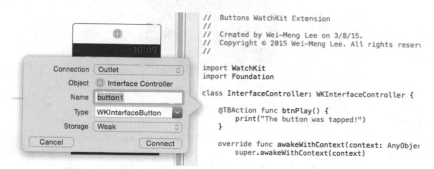

Figure 3.7   Creating an outlet for the button

2. This creates an outlet in the InterfaceController.swift file:

```
import WatchKit
import Foundation

class InterfaceController: WKInterfaceController {

    @IBOutlet var button1: WKInterfaceButton!

    @IBAction func btnPlay() {
        print("The button was tapped!")
    }
```

3. Add the following statements in bold to the InterfaceController.swift file:

```
override func awakeWithContext(context: AnyObject?) {
    super.awakeWithContext(context)

    // Configure interface objects here.
    button1.setTitle("Play Video")
}
```

> **Note**
>
> Observe that, while you can change the title of a button, you cannot get the title of the button programmatically.

4. Select the WatchKit App scheme and run the project on the Apple Watch Simulator. You should now see the title of the button changed to "Play Video" (see Figure 3.8).

Figure 3.8   Changing the title of the button dynamically

Displaying Attributed Strings

The Button control supports *attributed strings*. Attributed strings allow you to specify different attributes (such as color, font, size, etc.) for different parts of a string. In the following steps, you display the title of the button using different colors:

1. Add the following statements in bold to the InterfaceController.swift file:

```
override func awakeWithContext(context: AnyObject?) {
    super.awakeWithContext(context)

    // Configure interface objects here.

    // button1.setTitle("Play Video")
    let str = NSMutableAttributedString(
        string: "Hello, Apple Watch!")
```

```
//------display the Hello in yellow---
str.addAttribute(NSForegroundColorAttributeName,
    value: UIColor.yellowColor(),
    range: NSMakeRange(0, 5))

//---display the , in red---
str.addAttribute(NSForegroundColorAttributeName,
    value: UIColor.redColor(),
    range: NSMakeRange(5, 1))

//---display Apple Watch! in green---
str.addAttribute(NSForegroundColorAttributeName,
    value: UIColor.greenColor(),
    range: NSMakeRange(7, 12))
button1.setAttributedTitle(str)
}
```

2. Select the WatchKit App scheme and run the project on the Apple Watch Simulator. You should see the title of the button displayed in multiple colors, as shown
   in Figure 3.9 (readers of the print book will not see the colors in the figure).

Figure 3.9   Displaying the button title with mixed colors

Using Custom Fonts

Using attributed strings, you can also use different fonts for parts of a string. To illus-
trate this, let's modify the example in the previous section to display part of the button's
title using a custom font.

For this example, use the Impact font that is installed on your Mac. The Impact font
is represented using the Impact.ttf file located in the /Library/Fonts/ folder.

1. Drag and drop a copy of the Impact.ttf file onto the Extension project in Xcode.

2. You are asked to choose a few options. Select the options shown in Figure 3.10.
   This adds the Impact.ttf file onto the Extension and WatchKit App projects.

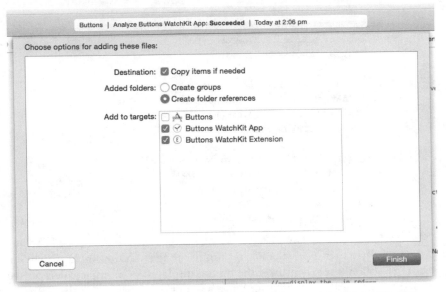

Figure 3.10   Adding the font file to the Extension and the WatchKit App

Note

Remember to add the font file to both the WatchKit Extension and WatchKit App. Also, be aware that adding custom fonts to the project adds considerable size and memory usage to your watch app. So, try to use the system font unless you have a very good reason not to.

3. Figure 3.11 shows the Impact.ttf file in the project.

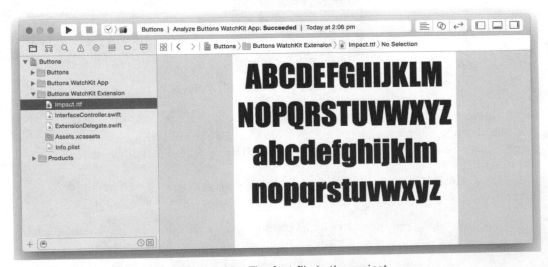

Figure 3.11   The font file in the project

4. Add a new key named **UIAppFonts** to the Info.plist file located in the Extension and set its Item 0 to **Impact.ttf** (see Figure 3.12).

> **Note**
>
> If your Info.plist file does not show the items as shown in Figure 3.12, simply right-click any of the items in it and select **Show Raw Keys/Values**.

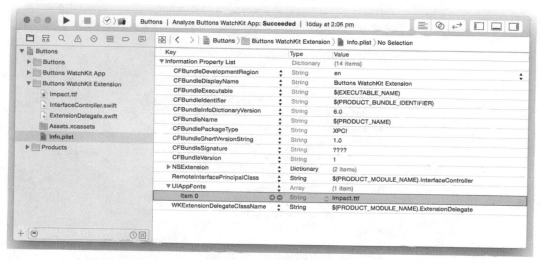

Figure 3.12   Specifying the font filename in the Extension project

5. Likewise, add a new key named **UIAppFonts** to the Info.plist file located in the WatchKit App and set its Item 0 to **Impact.ttf** (see Figure 3.13).

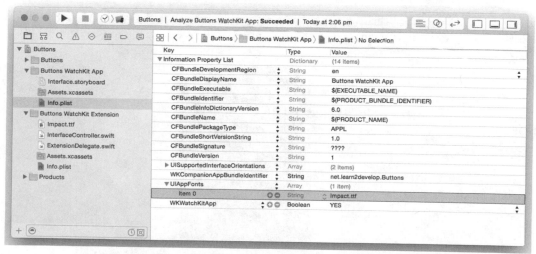

Figure 3.13   Specifying the font filename in the WatchKit app project

6. Add the following statements in bold to the InterfaceController.swift file:

```
override func awakeWithContext(context: AnyObject?) {
super.awakeWithContext(context)

// Configure interface objects here.
// button1.setTitle("Play Video")
let str = NSMutableAttributedString(
    string: "Hello, Apple Watch!")

//---display the Hello in yellow---
str.addAttribute(NSForegroundColorAttributeName,
    value: UIColor.yellowColor(),
    range: NSMakeRange(0, 5))

//---display Hello using the Impact font, size 22---
str.addAttribute(NSFontAttributeName,
    value: UIFont(name: "Impact", size: 22.0)!,
    range: NSMakeRange(0, 5))

//---display the , in red---
str.addAttribute(NSForegroundColorAttributeName,
    value: UIColor.redColor(),
    range: NSMakeRange(5, 1))

//---display Apple Watch! in green---
str.addAttribute(NSForegroundColorAttributeName,
    value: UIColor.greenColor(),
    range: NSMakeRange(7, 12))
button1.setAttributedTitle(str)
}
```

7. Select the WatchKit App scheme and run the project on the Apple Watch Simulator. You should now see "Hello" displayed using the Impact font (see Figure 3.14).

Figure 3.14   Displaying "Hello" using a custom font

Note

Once you have added a custom font to your project, you can use the font directly in Interface Builder by setting the Font attribute of a control to **Custom** and then selecting the font that you want to use in the Family attribute.

Getting the Font Name

One common problem in dealing with fonts is that the filename of the custom font that you are using is not always the same as the font name. The following code snippet allows you to print out the name of each font family and its corresponding font name:

```
for family in UIFont.familyNames() {
    print(family)
    for name in UIFont.fontNamesForFamilyName(family as String) {
    print("--\(name)")
    }
}
```

This code snippet prints the output as shown In Figure 3.15. For example, if you want to use the Helvetica Neue font, you have to specify in your code one of the font names printed: HelveticaNeue-Italic, HelveticaNeue-Bold, etc.

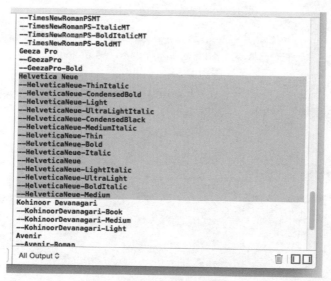

Figure 3.15   Printing out the font families and their associated font names

Changing the Background Image of Button

Besides displaying text, the Button control can also display a background image. The following exercise shows you how to add an image to the project and use it as the background of a button:

1. Drag and drop the image named play.png onto the Assets.xcassets item in the WatchKit App (see Figure 3.16).

> **Note**
>
> You can find a copy of this image in the source code download for this book.

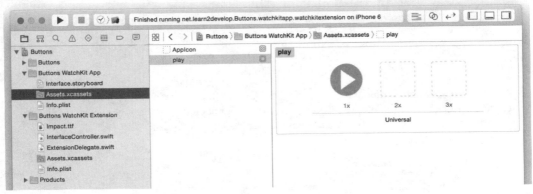

Figure 3.16   Adding an image to the project

2. In the Attributes Inspector window for the play.png image, check the watchOS checkbox (see Figure 3.17, right). Then, move the play.png into the box labeled

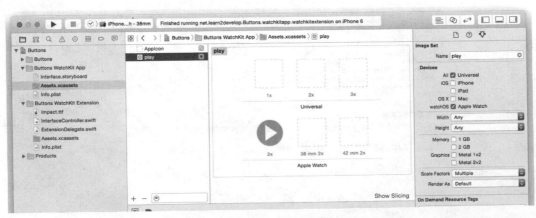

Figure 3.17   Specifying device-specific images to use

2× (see Figure 3.17, middle). This signifies that this image will be displayed for all sizes of Apple Watch. If you want to use different images for the 38mm Apple Watch and the 42mm Apple Watch, you can drag and drop different images onto the boxes labeled "38 mm 2×" and "42 mm 2×." For this example, you will use the same image for the two different watch sizes.

3. In the InterfaceController.swift file, add the following statements in bold:

```swift
override func awakeWithContext(context: AnyObject?) {
    super.awakeWithContext(context)

    // Configure interface objects here.
    // button1.setTitle("Play Video")

    /*
    let str = NSMutableAttributedString(
        string: "Hello, Apple Watch!")

    //---display the Hello in yellow---
    str.addAttribute(NSForegroundColorAttributeName,
        value: UIColor.yellowColor(),
        range: NSMakeRange(0, 5))

    //---display Hello using the Impact font, size 22---
    str.addAttribute(NSFontAttributeName,
        value: UIFont(name: "Impact", size: 22.0)!,
        range: NSMakeRange(0, 5))

    //---display the , in red---
    str.addAttribute(NSForegroundColorAttributeName,
        value: UIColor.redColor(),
        range: NSMakeRange(5, 1))

    //---display Apple Watch! in green---
    str.addAttribute(NSForegroundColorAttributeName,
        value: UIColor.greenColor(),
        range: NSMakeRange(7, 12))
    button1.setAttributedTitle(str)
    */

    button1.setBackgroundImageNamed("play")
}
```

4. Select the WatchKit App scheme and run the project on the Apple Watch Simulator. You should now see the image on the button (see Figure 3.18).

Figure 3.18   Displaying an image on the button

Do not use the `setBackgroundImage:` method by passing it a `UIImage` instance, like this:

```
button1.setBackgroundImage(UIImage(named: "play"))
```

This is because the `UIImage` class looks for the specified image (`"play"`) in the main bundle (the Extension). And because the play.png file is in the Watch-Kit App, the image cannot be found and, therefore, the image will not be set successfully.

5. You can also set the background image of the button in the storyboard via the Background attribute in the Attributes Inspector window.

Switch

The Switch control allows the user to toggle between the ON and OFF states. It is commonly used in cases where you allow users to enable or disable a particular setting. In the following example, you will create a project and see how the Switch control works:

1. Using Xcode, create a new iOS App with WatchKit App project and name it **Switches**. Uncheck the option Include Notification Scene so that we can keep the WatchKit project to a bare minimum.

2. Select the Interface.storyboard file to edit it in the Storyboard Editor.

3. Drag and drop a Switch control onto the default Interface Controller (see Figure 3.19).

4. In the Attributes Inspector window, set the Title attribute of the Switch control to **Aircon** (see Figure 3.20).

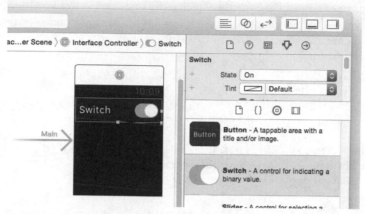

Figure 3.19   Adding a Switch control to the Interface Controller

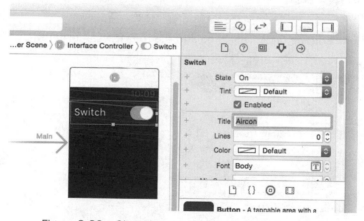

Figure 3.20   Changing the title of the Switch control

5. Add a Label control to the Interface Controller (see Figure 3.21).

Figure 3.21   Adding a Label control to the Interface Controller

6. Create an outlet for the Switch control and name it **switch**. Likewise, create an outlet for the Label control and name it **label**. Then, create an action for the Switch control and name it **switchAction**. The InterfaceController.swift file should now look like this:

```
import WatchKit
import Foundation

class InterfaceController: WKInterfaceController {

    @IBOutlet var `switch`: WKInterfaceSwitch!
    @IBOutlet var label: WKInterfaceLabel!
    @IBAction func switchAction(value: Bool) {
    }
```

> **Note**
>
> Because switch is a reserved word in the Swift programming language, if you try to use it as the name of an outlet, you have to enclose it with a pair of back quotes (``).

8. Add the following statements in bold to the InterfaceController.swift file:

```
    @IBAction func switchAction(value: Bool) {
        value ? label.setText("Aircon is on") :
            label.setText("Aircon is off")
    }

    override func awakeWithContext(context: AnyObject?) {
        super.awakeWithContext(context)

        // Configure interface objects here.
        `switch`.setOn(false)
        label.setText("")

    }
```

> **Note**
>
> You can programmatically set the value of a Switch control, but you will not be able to get its value. To know its value, you need to implement the action of the Switch control and save its value whenever its state changes.

9. Select the WatchKit App scheme and run the project on the Apple Watch Simulator. On the Apple Watch Simulator, click the Switch control to turn it on and off and observe the message printed in the Label control (see Figure 3.22).

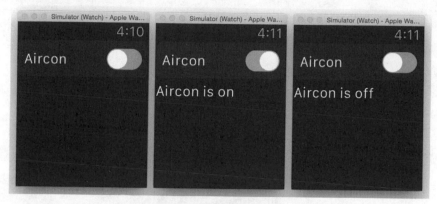

Figure 3.22   Testing the Switch control

Slider

The Slider control is a visual control with two buttons (– and +) that allow the user to decrement or increment a floating-point value. It is usually used in situations where you want the user to select from a range of values, such as the temperature settings in a thermostat or the volume of the iPhone.

1. Using Xcode, create a new iOS App with WatchKit App project and name it **Sliders**. Uncheck the option Include Notification Scene so that we can keep the WatchKit project to a bare minimum.
2. Select the Interface.storyboard file to edit it in the Storyboard Editor.
3. Drag and drop a Slider control onto the default Interface Controller (see Figure 3.23).

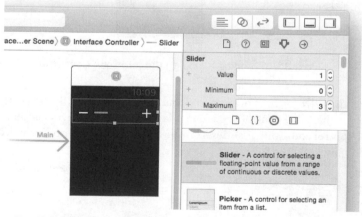

Figure 3.23   Adding a Slider control to the Interface Controller

4. Select the WatchKit App scheme and run the project on the Apple Watch Simulator. On the Apple Watch Simulator, click the + and − buttons (see Figure 3.24) and observe the slider.

Figure 3.24   Testing the slider

5. Add a Label control to the Interface Controller (see Figure 3.25).

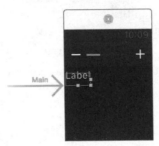

Figure 3.25   Adding a label to the Interface Controller

6. Create an outlet for the Slider control and name it **slider**. Likewise, create an outlet for the Label control and name it **label**. Then, create an action for the Slider control and name it **sliderAction**. The InterfaceController.swift file should now look like this:

```
import WatchKit
import Foundation
```

```
class InterfaceController: WKInterfaceController {

    @IBOutlet var slider: WKInterfaceSlider!
    @IBOutlet var label: WKInterfaceLabel!

    @IBAction func sliderAction(value: Float) {
    }
```

7. Set the attributes for the Slider control as follows (see Figure 3.26):

   Maximum: **10**

   Steps: **5**

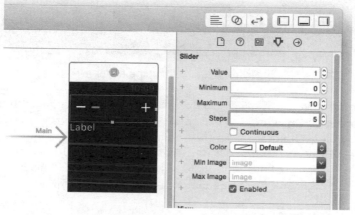

Figure 3.26   Setting the attributes for the Slider control

8. Add the following statements in bold to the InterfaceController.swift file:

```
@IBAction func sliderAction(value: Float) {
    label.setText("\(value)")
}

override func awakeWithContext(context: AnyObject?) {
    super.awakeWithContext(context)

    // Configure interface objects here.
    slider.setValue(0.0)
    label.setText("0.0")
}
```

> **Note**
>
> You can programmatically set the value of a Slider control, but you will not be able to get its value. To know its value, you need to implement the action of the Slider control and save its value whenever the value changes.

9. Select the WatchKit App scheme and run the project on the Apple Watch Simulator. Click the – and + buttons and observe the value printed on the Label control (see Figure 3.27).

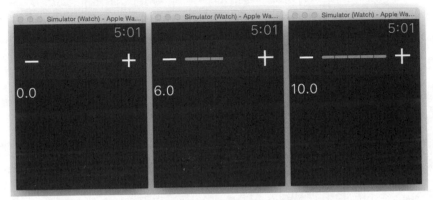

Figure 3.27   Testing the slider

The Steps attribute specifies how many times you can click the slider to reach its maximum value. The increment or decrement value of the slider at any point is dependent on the length of the slider (Maximum value minus Minimum value) divided by the value of Steps. In this example, the length of the slider is 10 (maximum of 10 minus minimum of 0) and the value of Steps is 5; hence, the slider increments or decrements by 2 whenever the + or – button is clicked.

Alerts and Action Sheets

In watchOS 2, Apple now allows developers to display alerts and actions just like they did in iPhone and iPad:

1. Using Xcode, create a new iOS App with WatchKit App project and name it **UsingAlerts**. Uncheck the option Include Notification Scene so that we can keep the WatchKit project to a bare minimum.

2. Select the Interface.storyboard file to edit it in the Storyboard Editor.

3. Drag and drop a Button control onto the default Interface Controller (see Figure 3.28) and set its title to **Show Alerts**.

4. Create an action for the Button control and name it **btnShowAlerts**. The InterfaceController.swift file should now look like this:

```
import WatchKit
import Foundation

class InterfaceController: WKInterfaceController {

    @IBAction func btnShowAlerts() {
    }
```

Figure 3.28   Adding a button to the Interface Controller

5. Add the following statements in bold to the InterfaceController.swift file:

```
import WatchKit
import Foundation

class InterfaceController: WKInterfaceController {

    func performAction(actionStyle: WKAlertActionStyle) {
        switch actionStyle {
        case .Default:
            print("OK")
        case .Cancel:
            print("Cancel")
        case .Destructive:
            print("Destructive")
        }
    }

    @IBAction func btnShowAlerts() {
        let okAction = WKAlertAction(title: "OK",
            style: WKAlertActionStyle.Default) { () -> Void in
                self.performAction(WKAlertActionStyle.Default)
        }

        let cancelAction = WKAlertAction(title: "Cancel",
            style: WKAlertActionStyle.Cancel) { () -> Void in
                self.performAction(WKAlertActionStyle.Cancel)
        }

        let abortAction = WKAlertAction(title: "Abort",
            style: WKAlertActionStyle.Destructive) { () -> Void in
                self.performAction(WKAlertActionStyle.Destructive)
        }
```

```
presentAlertControllerWithTitle("Title",
    message: "Message",
    preferredStyle: WKAlertControllerStyle.Alert,
    actions: [okAction, cancelAction, abortAction])
}
```

Here, you first defined a function named `performAction:` that prints out a message depending on the style that is passed in as the argument. Next, in the `btnShowAlerts` action, you created three `WKAlertAction` instances, each with a specific style (`Default`, `Cancel`, and `Destructive`). Within each instance, you have a closure that is fired when the user clicks on the action buttons. When each button is clicked, you simply call the `performAction:` function to print out a message so that you know which button was clicked. Finally, you called the `presentAlertControllerWithTitle:message:preferredStyle:actions:` method to display an alert, together with the three action buttons.

6. Select the WatchKit App scheme and run the project on the Apple Watch Simulator. Clicking the button displays an alert (see Figure 3.29).

Figure 3.29   Displaying an alert in the Apple Watch

> **Note**
>
> Note that the **Abort** button in the alert is displayed in red as its style is set to `Destructive`.

7. Modify the `presentAlertControllerWithTitle:message:preferred-Style:actions:` method, as follows:

```
//---SideBySideButtonsAlert supports exactly two actions---
presentAlertControllerWithTitle("Title",
    message: "Message",
    preferredStyle:
        WKAlertControllerStyle.SideBySideButtonsAlert,
    actions: [okAction, cancelAction])
```

8. Select the WatchKit App scheme and run the project on the Apple Watch Simulator. Clicking the button displays an alert with the two buttons displayed side by side (see Figure 3.30).

Figure 3.30   Displaying an alert with two buttons side by side in the Apple Watch

> **Note**
>
> For the `SideBySideButtonsAlert` style, you need to specify exactly two action buttons.

9. Modify the `presentAlertControllerWithTitle:message:preferred-Style:actions:` method as follows:

```
presentAlertControllerWithTitle("Title",
    message: "Message",
    preferredStyle: WKAlertControllerStyle.ActionSheet,
    actions: [okAction, cancelAction, abortAction])
```

10. Select the WatchKit App scheme and run the project on the Apple Watch Simulator. Clicking the button displays an alert, as shown in Figure 3.31.

> **Note**
>
> When using the `ActionSheet` style, the action button that is set to the `Cancel` style is displayed at the top-left corner of the screen. Even if you do not specify the cancel action button, a default **Cancel** button is still displayed to close the action sheet (though in this case you cannot handle the event that is fired when the user taps the **Cancel** button).

Figure 3.31   Displaying an action sheet in the Apple Watch

Summary

In this chapter, you looked at the various controls that you can use to build the UI of your Apple Watch application. In particular, you saw the various controls that you can interact with by using the tap gesture, such as the Button, Switch, and Slider controls. In addition, you learned about the new alerts and action sheets that you can use to display information in watchOS 2. In the next chapter, you learn more about the other controls that primarily display information to the user.

Displaying and Gathering Information

Innovation distinguishes between a leader and a follower.
Steve Jobs

In the previous chapter, you saw the various controls with which the user interacts through the tap gesture. In this chapter, you continue to explore the controls available in the WatchKit framework. This time you focus on controls that display information, as well as controls that gather information.

Displaying Information

To display information to the user on the Apple Watch, the WatchKit provides the following controls:

- **Label**: A control that displays formatted text whose content can be changed dynamically.
- **Image**: A control that displays a single image or a series of images (for animation).
- **Table**: A control that displays a list of data. Only single-column tables are supported at this moment.
- **Picker**: A new control in watchOS 2, the Picker control shows a list of items just like the Table control, but with some nice animations.
- **Movie**: Another new control in watchOS 2, the Movie control provides a UI for playing media files.

Label

You have already used the Label control in a number of projects. As you have seen, the Label control displays a string of text. Like the Button control, the Label control also supports attributed strings.

> **Note**
>
> Refer to the section "Displaying Attributed Strings" in Chapter 3, "Responding to User Actions," for more information on attributed strings.

We discuss more about the Label control in Chapter 7, "Interfacing with iOS Apps," where you learn about the strategy to internationalize and localize your Apple Watch applications.

Image

You can use images in several places:

- As the background of an Interface Controller
- As the background of a button (discussed in the section on buttons)
- Independently using the Image control

Setting the Background of an Interface Controller

Let's first learn how to change the background of the Interface Controller to display an image:

1. Using Xcode, create a new iOS App with WatchKit App project and name it **Images**. Uncheck the option Include Notification Scene so that we can keep the WatchKit project to a bare minimum.

2. Drag and drop two images named flag.png and apple.png to the Assets.xcassets file in the WatchKit App (see Figure 4.1). Ensure that you moved them to the 2× section of the Apple Watch category.

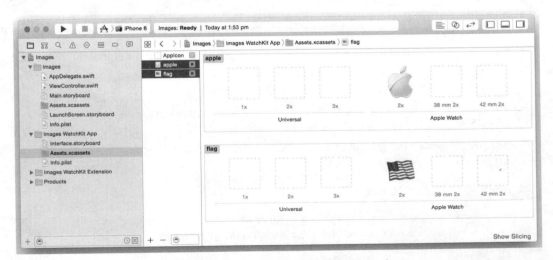

Figure 4.1   Adding an image to the project

> **Note**
>
> Chapter 3 showed how to move an image in the Assets.xcassets file into the 2× section of the Apple Watch category. You can find a copy of the images used here in the source code download for this book.

3. Select the Interface.storyboard file to edit it in the Storyboard Editor.

4. In the default Interface Controller, set the Background attribute to **apple** (see Figure 4.2) and set its Mode attribute to **Aspect Fit**. The image will be displayed as the background for the Interface Controller.

Figure 4.2   Setting the background image for the Interface Controller

5. Select the WatchKit App scheme and run the project on the Apple Watch Simulator. You should see the image (see Figure 4.3).

Figure 4.3   The Interface Controller showing
the image in the background

Using the Image Control

The previous section showed how the Interface Controller can display an image as its background. In this section, you learn how to use the Image control to display an image on the Interface Controller.

1. Using the same project created in the previous section, add an Image control onto the Interface Controller (see Figure 4.4). Set its Horizontal and Vertical attributes to **Center**.

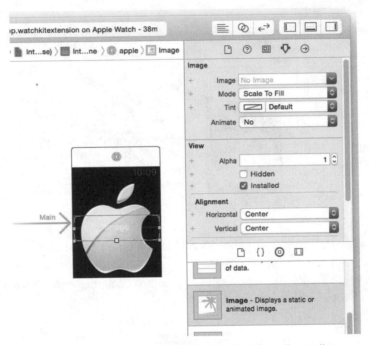

Figure 4.4   Adding an image to the Interface Controller

2. Set its Image attribute to **flag** (see Figure 4.5) and Mode attribute to **Scale To Fill**.

3. Select the WatchKit App scheme and run the project on the Apple Watch Simulator. You should see the image (see Figure 4.6).

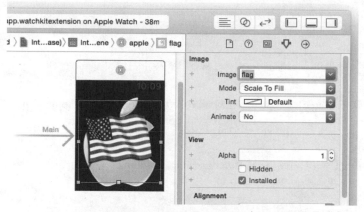

Figure 4.5   Setting the image for the Image control

Figure 4.6   View the image displayed in the Image control

4. You can also programmatically set the image in the Image control using the setImageNamed: method of the Image control. To do that, create an outlet for the Image control and add the following statements in bold to the InterfaceController .swift file:

```swift
import WatchKit
import Foundation

class InterfaceController: WKInterfaceController {

    @IBOutlet var image: WKInterfaceImage!
```

```
override func awakeWithContext(context: AnyObject?) {
    super.awakeWithContext(context)

    // Configure interface objects here.
    image.setImageNamed("flag")
}
```

5. Select the WatchKit App scheme and run the project on the Apple Watch Simulator. You should see the image displayed as before.

> **Note**
>
> For this step, you need to clear the Image attribute for the Image control, which was previously set to **flag** in Step 2.

Performing Animation

In the Apple Watch, animations are performed using a series of static images. These images are stored in the WatchKit app bundle so that they can be presented quickly to the user. In this section, you learn how to perform simple animations using the Image control:

1. Using the same project created in the previous section, drag and drop a series of images to the Assets.xcassets file in the WatchKit App (see Figure 4.7). Ensure that you moved them to the 2× section of the Apple Watch category.

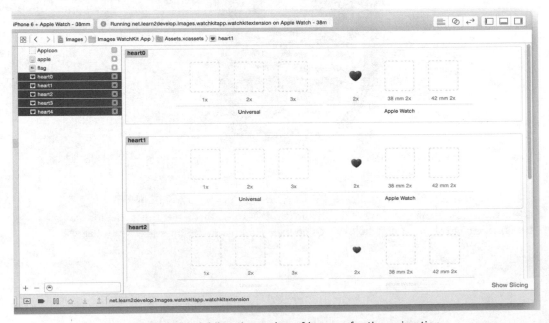

Figure 4.7   Adding the series of images for the animation

> **Note**
>
> You can find a copy of the images in the source code download for this book.

The images should be named and sized as follows:

Image Name	Size
heart0.png	130×113 pixels
heart1.png	110×96 pixels
heart2.png	90×78 pixels
heart3.png	70×61 pixels
heart4.png	50×43 pixels

2. Set the Mode attribute of the Image control in the Interface Controller to **Center** (see Figure 4.8).

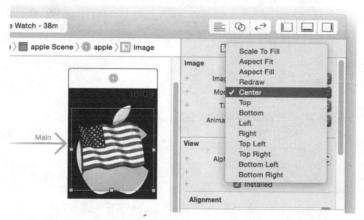

Figure 4.8   Setting the display mode for the Image control

3. Add the following statements in bold to the InterfaceController.swift file:

```
override func awakeWithContext(context: AnyObject?) {
    super.awakeWithContext(context)

    // Configure interface objects here.
    image.setImageNamed("heart")

    //---use 5 images, change every 0.5 seconds,
    //---location is the starting image - 0 for heart0.png, length is
    // for number of images to animate---
    image.startAnimatingWithImagesInRange(
```

```
              NSRange(location:0, length:5),
              duration: 0.5, repeatCount: Int.max)
    }
```

4. Select the WatchKit App scheme and run the project on the Apple Watch Simulator. You should see a throbbing heart (see Figure 4.9).

Figure 4.9   The animation of the throbbing heart

Table

In an Apple Watch application, you use a Table control to display a list of items. For example, you might want to display a list of names on your Apple Watch. Tables are not limited to displaying text; you can also display images on each row. In fact, each row can be configured to display a combination of the different controls that we cover in this chapter and the preceding one.

1. Using Xcode, create a new iOS App with WatchKit App project and name it **Tables**. Uncheck the option Include Notification Scene so that we can keep the WatchKit project to a bare minimum.

2. Select the Interface.storyboard file located in the Tables WatchKit App to edit it in the Storyboard Editor.

3. Add a Table control to the Interface Controller (see Figure 4.10).

4. Add a Label control onto the Table control, as shown in Figure 4.11.

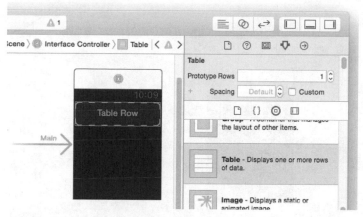

Figure 4.10   Adding a Table control to the Interface Controller

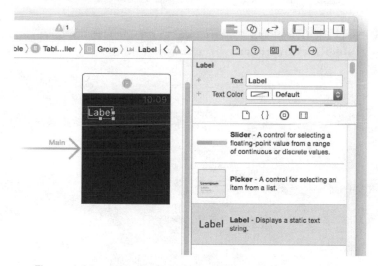

Figure 4.11   Adding a Label control onto the Table control

5. Select the Label control and set its Horizontal and Vertical attributes to **Center**
(see Figure 4.12). This makes the Label control appear in the center of the Table
control.

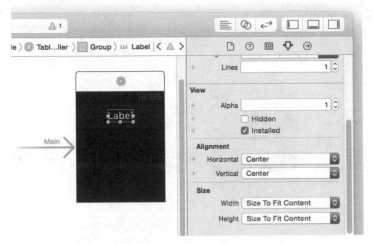

Figure 4.12   Setting the attributes for the Label control

6. Add a Swift file (**watchOS | Swift File**) to the Extension project and name it **FruitsTableRowController.swift** (see Figure 4.13).

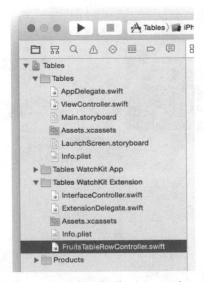

Figure 4.13   Adding a Swift class to the project

7. Populate the FruitsTableRowController.swift file with the following:

```
import Foundation
import WatchKit
```

```
class FruitsTableRowController: NSObject {
    @IBOutlet weak var label: WKInterfaceLabel!
}
```

8. Back in the Storyboard Editor, select the Table Row Controller (see Figure 4.14, top) and then set its Class to **FruitsTableRowController**. The Table Row Controller is now named Fruits Table Row Controller.

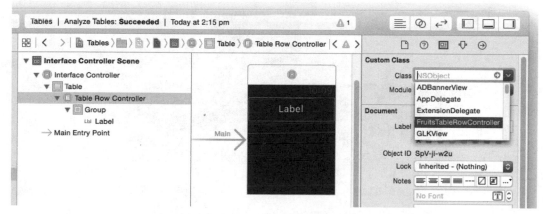

Figure 4.14   Assigning the Table control to the Swift class

9. Select the Fruits Table Row Controller and then set its Identifier attribute to **FruitsTableRowControllerID** (see Figure 4.15). The Fruits Table Row Controller is now named FruitsTableRowControllerID.

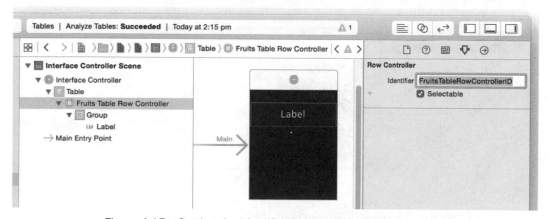

Figure 4.15   Setting the Identifier for the Table Row Controller

10. Right-click **FruitsTableRowControllerID** and, in the popup, connect the label outlet to the Label control on the table (see Figure 4.16).

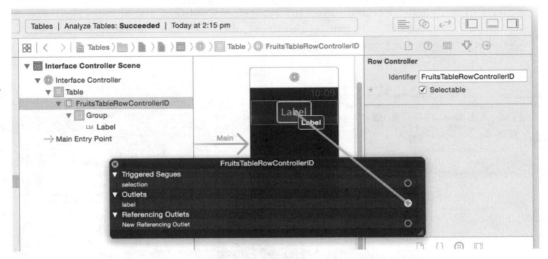

Figure 4.16   Connecting the outlet to the Label control

11. Click the **View | Assistant Editor | Show Assistant Editor** menu item to reveal the Code Editor. Control-click the Table control (see Figure 4.17) and drag and drop it over the InterfaceController class.

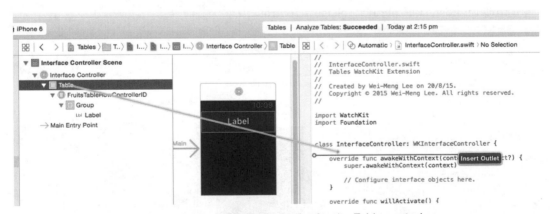

Figure 4.17   Creating an outlet for the Table control

12. Name the outlet **table** (see Figure 4.18) and click **Connect**.

```
//
// ᴛɑᴜ᷉ᴛᴇʂ ᴡɑᴛᴄʜᴋɪᴛ ᴇxᴛᴇɴʂɪᴏɴ
//
// Created by Wei-Meng Lee on 20/8/15.
// Copyright © 2015 Wei-Meng Lee. All rights reserved.
//

import WatchKit
import Foundation

class InterfaceController: WKInterfaceController {

    override func awakeWithContext(context: AnyObject?) {
        super.awakeWithContext(context)

        // Configure interface objects here.
    }

    override func willActivate() {
        // This method is called when watch view controller
```

Figure 4.18   Naming the outlet

13. Add the following statements in bold to the InterfaceController.swift file:

```
import WatchKit
import Foundation

class InterfaceController: WKInterfaceController {

    @IBOutlet var table: WKInterfaceTable!

    var fruits = [
        "Durian",
        "Pineapple",
        "Apple",
        "Orange",
        "Guava",
        "Peach",
        "Rambutan" ]

    func populateTable() {
        table.setNumberOfRows(fruits.count,
        withRowType: "FruitsTableRowControllerID")

        for (index, value) in fruits.enumerate() {
            let row = table.rowControllerAtIndex(index) as!
                FruitsTableRowController
            row.label.setText(value)
        }
    }

    override func awakeWithContext(context: AnyObject?) {
        super.awakeWithContext(context)

        // Configure interface objects here.
        populateTable()
    }
```

14. Select the WatchKit App scheme and run the project on the Apple Watch Simulator. You should now see a list of fruits on the Apple Watch Simulator (see Figure 4.19).

Figure 4.19   The Table control displaying a list of items

Displaying Images

Instead of displaying text in the Table control, it is often more useful to display images next to the text:

1. Add an image named fruit.png to the Assets.xcassets file in the WatchKit App of the project (see Figure 4.20). Be sure to move the image into the 2× box of the Apple Watch section.

> **Note**
> You can find a copy of the image in the source code download for this book.

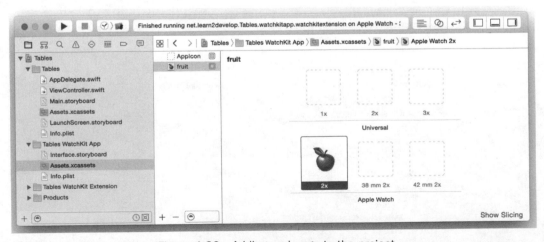

Figure 4.20   Adding an image to the project

2. Add an Image control onto the Table control, as shown in Figure 4.21.

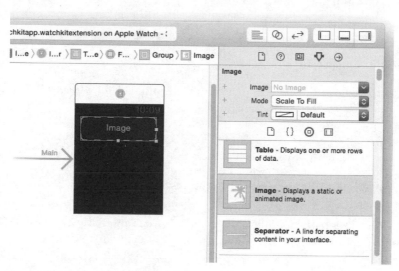

Figure 4.21   Adding an Image control to the Table control

3. Set the attributes of the Image control as follows (see Figure 4.22):

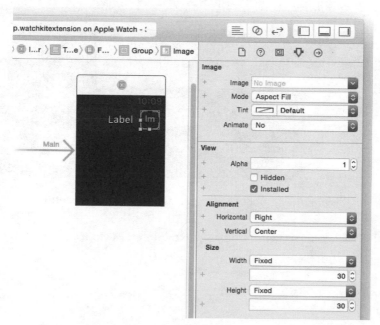

Figure 4.22   Setting the attributes for the Image control

Mode: **Aspect Fill**

Horizontal: **Right**

Vertical: **Center**

Width: **Fixed | 30**

Height: **Fixed | 30**

4. Add the following statement in bold to the FruitsTableRowController.swift file:

```
import Foundation
import WatchKit

class FruitsTableRowController: NSObject {
    @IBOutlet weak var label: WKInterfaceLabel!
    @IBOutlet weak var image: WKInterfaceImage!
}
```

5. Back in the Storyboard Editor, right-click **FruitsTableRowControllerID** and connect the image outlet to the Image control (see Figure 4.23).

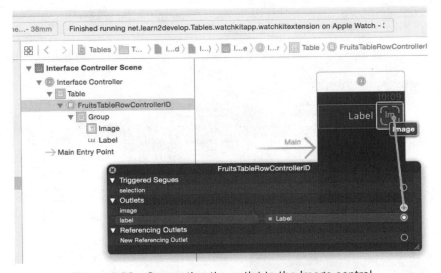

Figure 4.23   Connecting the outlet to the Image control

6. Add the following statements in bold to the InterfaceController.swift file:

```
func populateTable() {
    table.setNumberOfRows(fruits.count,
    withRowType: "FruitsTableRowControllerID")
```

```
        for (index, value) in fruits.enumerate() {
            let row = table.rowControllerAtIndex(index) as!
                FruitsTableRowController
            row.label.setText(value)
            row.image.setImageNamed("fruit")
        }
    }
```

7. Select the WatchKit App scheme and run the project on the Apple Watch Simulator. You should see the image displayed next to each row in the Table control (see Figure 4.24).

Figure 4.24   The Table control with the image displayed for each row

Selecting an Item in a Table

When an item in the Table control is tapped, the `table:didSelectRowAtIndex:` method fires.

> **Note**
>
> If you simply want to use the Table control to display a list of information and not make the individual rows tappable, uncheck the Selectable attribute of the Row Controller as shown in Figure 4.15.

You need to implement this method if you want to perform an action when an item is selected, such as navigating to another Interface Controller:

1. Add the following statements in bold to the InterfaceController.swift file:

```
import WatchKit
import Foundation
```

```
class InterfaceController: WKInterfaceController {

    @IBOutlet var table: WKInterfaceTable!

    var fruits = [
        "Durian",
        "Pineapple",
        "Apple",
        "Orange",
        "Guava",
        "Peach",
        "Rambutan" ]

    override func table(table: WKInterfaceTable,
        didSelectRowAtIndex rowIndex: Int) {
        print(fruits[rowIndex])
    }
}
```

2. Select the WatchKit App scheme and run the project on the Apple Watch Simu-
    lator. Click an item and observe that the Output window displays the name of the
    fruit selected (see Figure 4.25).

Figure 4.25   Clicking a row displays the name of the item

Picker

The Picker control is a new control introduced in watchOS 2. Like the Table control,
the Picker control displays a list of items for the user to choose from. Unlike the Table
control, the user interacts with the Picker control solely through the Digital Crown; the
Picker control does not allow the user to scroll through the list using touch. In addition,
the Picker control provides animation of items when the user scrolls through them.

The following examples demonstrate the use of the new Picker control.

Displaying a List of Text

Let's start by displaying a list of text items in a Picker control:

1. Using Xcode, create a new iOS App with WatchKit App project and name it UsingPicker. Uncheck the option Include Notification Scene so that we can keep the WatchKit project to a bare minimum.

2. Select the Interface.storyboard file to edit it in the Storyboard Editor.

3. Drag and drop a Picker control and a Button control onto the default Interface Controller (see Figure 4.26) and set the button's title to **Select**.

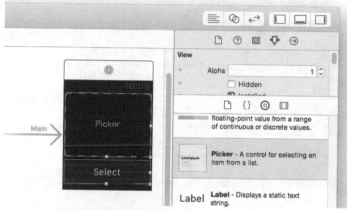

Figure 4.26   Adding a Picker and a Button control to the Interface Controller

4. Create an action for the Button and Picker controls and create an outlet for the Picker control. The InterfaceController.swift file should now look like this:

```
import WatchKit
import Foundation

class InterfaceController: WKInterfaceController {

    @IBOutlet var picker: WKInterfacePicker!

    @IBAction func btnPickerItemSelected(value: Int) {
    }

    @IBAction func btnSelect() {
    }
```

5. Add the following statements in bold to the InterfaceController.swift file:

```
import WatchKit
import Foundation
```

```
class InterfaceController: WKInterfaceController {
    var pickerIndex = 0
    let presidents = [
        "Dwight D. Eisenhower", "John F. Kennedy",
        "Lyndon B. Johnson", "Richard Nixon", "Gerald Ford",
        "Jimmy Carter", "Ronald Reagan", "George H. W. Bush",
        "Bill Clinton", "George W. Bush", "Barack Obama"
    ]

    @IBOutlet var picker: WKInterfacePicker!

    @IBAction func btnPickerItemSelected(value: Int) {
        pickerIndex = value
    }

    @IBAction func btnSelect() {
        print(presidents[pickerIndex])
    }

    override func awakeWithContext(context: AnyObject?) {
        super.awakeWithContext(context)

        // Configure interface objects here.

        //---array of WKPickerItem objects---
        var items = [WKPickerItem]()
        for (index, president) in presidents.enumerate() {
            let item = WKPickerItem()
            item.title = president
            items.append(item)
        }
        picker.setItems(items)
    }
}
```

The presidents array contains the list of presidents' names that you want to
display in the Picker control. Whenever the Picker control turns to display an item,
it fires the btnPickerItemSelected action, which in this case saves the index
of the item selected. When the user taps on the **Select** button, this index prints
the name of the president selected. To populate the Picker control with the list of
presidents' names, you iterate through the presidents array and then create an
array of WKPickerItem objects and assign it to the Picker control.

6. Select the WatchKit App scheme and run the project on the Apple Watch Simu-
    lator. You can scroll through the items in the Picker by using the scroll wheel on
    your mouse, or use two fingers to swipe on your Mac trackpad (see Figure 4.27).
    On a real Apple Watch, you interact with the Picker control using the Digital Crown.
    Clicking the **Select** button prints the name of the president in the Output
    window.

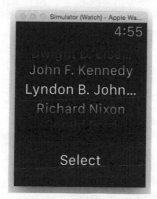

Figure 4.27 The Picker displaying
a list of presidents' names

Displaying Images

Besides text, the Picker control can also display images. Let's see how this is done:

1. Using the same project created in the previous section, drag and drop 11 images onto the Assets.xcassets item in the WatchKit app (see Figure 4.28). Be sure to move each image into the 2× box of the Apple Watch section.

> **Note**
>
> The images are available in the source code download for this book.

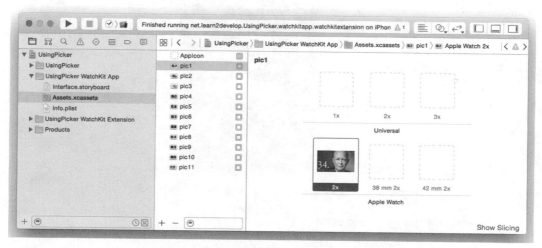

Figure 4.28 Adding the images to the Assets.xcassets file
[Images from https://www.whitehouse.gov/1600/Presidents]

2. Add the following statements in bold to the InterfaceController.swift file:

```
override func awakeWithContext(context: AnyObject?) {
    super.awakeWithContext(context)

    // Configure interface objects here.

    //---array of WKPickerItem objects---
    var items = [WKPickerItem]()
    for (index, president) in presidents.enumerate() {
        let item = WKPickerItem()
        item.title = president
        let image = WKImage(imageName: "pic\(index+1)")
        item.accessoryImage = image
        items.append(item)
    }
    picker.setItems(items)
}
```

The `WKImage` class takes the name of the image as its initializer. To assign an image to the items in the Picker control, you assign a `WKImage` object to each `WKPickerItem` object.

3. Select the WatchKit App scheme and run the project on the Apple Watch Simulator. You should now see the image displayed next to the text in the Picker control (see Figure 4.29).

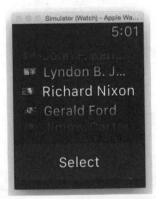

Figure 4.29   Adding pictures to the items in the Picker

Changing the Scrolling Style

The Picker control supports a number of styles that affect the way items are switched when the user scrolls through them. The following example shows you how to make the image fill up the Picker control and make the images transition like a Rolodex:

1. Using the same project created in the previous section, add the following statements in bold to the InterfaceController.swift file:

```
override func awakeWithContext(context: AnyObject?) {
    super.awakeWithContext(context)

    // Configure interface objects here.

    //---array of WKPickerItem objects---
    var items = [WKPickerItem]()
    for (index, president) in presidents.enumerate() {
        let item = WKPickerItem()
        item.title = president
        let image = WKImage(imageName: "pic\(index+1)")
        item.accessoryImage = image
        item.contentImage = image
        items.append(item)
    }
    picker.setItems(items)
}
```

To make the image fill the entire Picker control, set the `contentImage` property of the `WKPickerItem` object to the image.

2. In the Interface.storyboard file, set the Style attribute of the Picker control to **Stack** (see Figure 4.30).

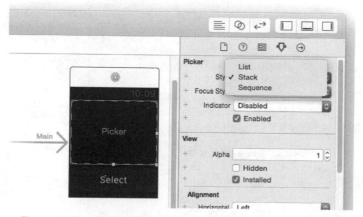

Figure 4.30   Setting the style of the Picker control to **Stack**

3. Select the WatchKit App scheme and run the project on the Apple Watch Simulator. The images in the Picker control will now scroll like a Rolodex (see Figure 4.31).

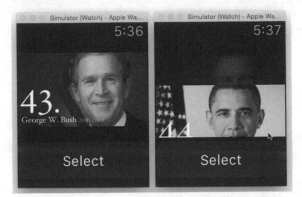

Figure 4.31   The Picker control behaving like a Rolodex

Displaying a Caption

When images occupy the entire Picker control, it is often useful to display a caption on top of each image. The following example shows you how to accomplish this:

1. Using the same project created in the previous section, add the following statements in bold to the InterfaceController.swift file:

```
override func awakeWithContext(context: AnyObject?) {
    super.awakeWithContext(context)

    // Configure interface objects here.

    //---array of WKPickerItem objects---
    var items = [WKPickerItem]()
    for (index, president) in presidents.enumerate() {
        let item = WKPickerItem()
        item.title = president

        let image = WKImage(imageName: "pic\(index+1)")
        item.accessoryImage = image

        item.caption = president
        item.contentImage = image
        items.append(item)
    }
    picker.setItems(items)
}
```

To display the name of the president on top of the image, set the `caption` property of the `WKPickerItem` object to the president's name.

2. In the Interface.storyboard file, set the Focus Style attribute to **Outline With Caption** (see Figure 4.32).

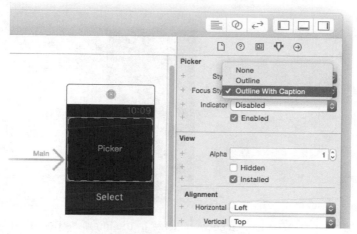

Figure 4.32   Setting the Focus Style of the Picker to **Outline With Caption**

3. Select the WatchKit App scheme and run the project on the Apple Watch Simulator. Scroll the images in the Picker control and observe the name of the president displayed above the image (see Figure 4.33).

Figure 4.33   The name of the president
displayed above the picture

Displaying a Control Knob

Because the Picker view interacts with the user through the Digitial Crown, you can make use of this feature and implement a control-knob-style UI on your watch app. The following shows you how:

1. In the Interface.storyboard file, drag and drop another Picker control onto the default Interface Controller (see Figure 4.34).

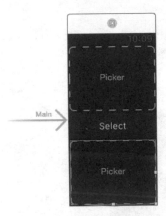

Figure 4.34   Adding a second Picker to the Interface Controller

2. Select the Picker control that you have just added and set its Style attribute to **Sequence** and its Focus Style attribute to **Outline With Caption**.

3. Create an outlet for this second Picker control and name it **picker2**. The InterfaceController.swift file should now look like this:

```
import WatchKit
import Foundation

class InterfaceController: WKInterfaceController {

    var pickerIndex = 0

    @IBOutlet var picker: WKInterfacePicker!
    @IBOutlet var picker2: WKInterfacePicker!
```

4. Prepare a set of images as shown in Figure 4.35 and name them **control0.png**, **control1.png**, **control2.png**, **control3.png**, and **control4.png**, respectively.

> **Note**
> You can find these images in the source code download for this book.

Figure 4.35   The series of images depicting the various states of a control knob

5. Drag and drop the images that you have prepared in the previous step into the Assets.xcassets file in the WatchKit app (see Figure 4.36). Be sure to move each image into the 2× box of the Apple Watch section.

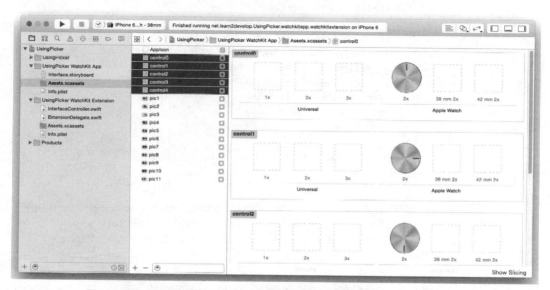

Figure 4.36   Adding the series of images to the Assets.xcassets file

6. Add the following statements in bold to the InterfaceController.swift file:

```
override func awakeWithContext(context: AnyObject?) {
    super.awakeWithContext(context)

    // Configure interface objects here.

    //---array of WKPickerItem objects---
    var items = [WKPickerItem]()

    for (index, president) in presidents.enumerate() {
        let item = WKPickerItem()
        item.title = president

        let image = WKImage(imageName: "pic\(index+1)")
        item.accessoryImage = image

        //---focus style set to Outline with Caption---
        //---style must be set to Stack---
        item.caption = president
        item.contentImage = image
```

```
        items.append(item)
    }
    picker.setItems(items)

    var items2 = [WKPickerItem]()
    for i in 0...4 {
        let item = WKPickerItem()
        let image = WKImage(imageName: "control\(i)")
        //---focus style set to Outline with Caption---
        //---style must be set to Sequence---
        item.caption = "\(( Double(i) / 4) * 100)%"
        item.contentImage = image
        items2.append(item)
    }
    picker2.setItems(items2)
    picker2.focus()

}
```

7. Select the WatchKit App scheme and run the project on the Apple Watch Simulator. Scroll the screen upward (observe that the second Picker control is already in focus) and use the scroll wheel (or trackpad) to turn the knob (see Figure 4.37).

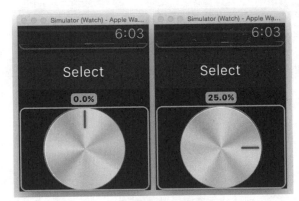

Figure 4.37   The control knob in action

Playing Media Files

In watchOS 2, developers are now able to play media (such as sound or video files) on the Apple Watch. There are two ways to do this: either programmatically or through the use of the Movie control.

Playing a Movie Programmatically

Let's see how you can play a media file programmatically:

1. Using Xcode, create a new iOS App with WatchKit App project and name it **Movies**. Uncheck the option Include Notification Scene so that we can keep the WatchKit project to a bare minimum.

2. Select the Interface.storyboard file to edit it in the Storyboard Editor.

3. Drag and drop a Button control onto the default Interface Controller and set its title to **Play** (see Figure 4.38).

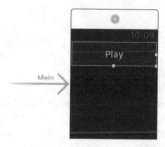

Figure 4.38   Adding a button to the Interface Controller

4. Drag and drop an MPEG file named sample_mpeg4.mp4 onto the Extension project (see Figure 4.39). Add it to the WatchKit Extension target.

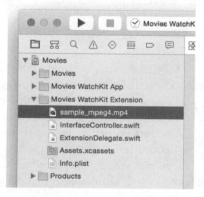

Figure 4.39   Adding a sample MPEG file to the Extension

> **Note**
>
> The sample_mpeg4.mp4 file is a free download from https://support.apple.com/en-us/HT201549.

5. Create an action in the InterfaceController.swift file and then connect it to the button:

```
import WatchKit
import Foundation

class InterfaceController: WKInterfaceController {

    @IBAction func btnPlay() {
    }
```

6. Add the following statements in bold to the InterfaceController.swift file:

```
import WatchKit
import Foundation

class InterfaceController: WKInterfaceController {

    @IBAction func btnPlay() {
        let bundle = NSBundle.mainBundle()
        if let url = bundle.URLForResource("sample_mpeg4",
            withExtension: "mp4") {
                let options =
                    [WKMediaPlayerControllerOptionsAutoplayKey: true]
                self.presentMediaPlayerControllerWithURL(url,
                    options: options) {
                    (didPlayToEnd, endTime, error) -> Void in
                    print("Movie finished playback")
                }
        } else {
            //---error handling---
            print("No movie found.")
        }
    }
```

You first create a dictionary containing the WKMediaPlayerController-OptionsAutoplayKey key with its value set to true (so that the media can start playing automatically when the media player controller interface is displayed). You then call the presentMediaPlayerControllerWithURL:options: method to display a modal interface for playing the media. When the user dismisses the media, or the media has finished playing, this method calls a completion block, where you can check to see if the media has played till the end, the amount of time the media has played, as well as any errors that occurred.

7. Select the WatchKit App scheme and run the project on the Apple Watch Simulator. Click the **Play** button and the video should play (see Figure 4.40).

Figure 4.40   Playing back the video programmatically

Playing a Movie Using the Movie Control

Instead of using a Button control to initiate the playback of media, the latest version of WatchKit comes with the new Movie control. The Movie control displays a **Play** button as well as an optional poster image.

1. Using the same project created in the previous section, add a Movie control onto the Interface Controller in the Interface.storyboard file (see Figure 4.41).

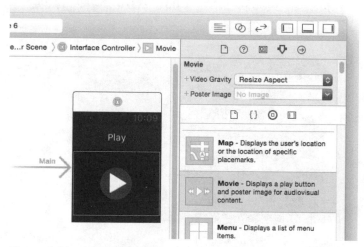

Figure 4.41   Adding the Movie control to the Interface Controller

2. Create an outlet for the Movie control in the InterfaceController.swift file:

```
import WatchKit
import Foundation
```

```
class InterfaceController: WKInterfaceController {

    @IBOutlet var movie: WKInterfaceMovie!

    @IBAction func btnPlay() {
        ...
    }
```

3. Add the following statements in bold to the InterfaceController.swift file:

```
override func awakeWithContext(context: AnyObject?) {
    super.awakeWithContext(context)

    // Configure interface objects here.
    let bundle = NSBundle.mainBundle()
    if let url = bundle.URLForResource("sample_mpeg4",
        withExtension: "mp4") {
        movie.setMovieURL(url)
    }
}
```

To associate the Movie control with a movie, call the setMovieURL method and pass it the URL of the movie. The movie to play must already be available on the Apple Watch (hence it needs to be bundled in your Extension).

4. Select the WatchKit App scheme and run the project on the Apple Watch Simulator. Click the Movie control and the video should play (see Figure 4.42).

Figure 4.42   Playing back the video using the Movie control

5. Drag and drop an image named posterimage.png onto the Assets.xcassets file in the WatchKit app (see Figure 4.43). Be sure to move each image into the 2× box of the Apple Watch section.

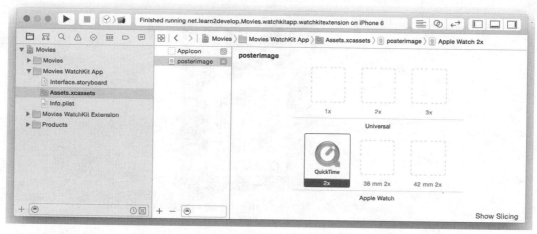

Figure 4.43   Adding a poster image to the Assets.xcassets file

6. Set the Poster Image attribute of the Movie control to **posterimage** (see Figure 4.44).

Figure 4.44   Setting the poster image for the Movie control

7. Select the WatchKit App scheme and run the project on the Apple Watch Simulator. You should now see the image displayed as the poster image for the Movie control (see Figure 4.45).

Figure 4.45   The Movie control displaying the poster image

Gathering Information

While the Apple Watch is more for consuming information, there are certainly times when it is necessary to obtain inputs from the users. Users can use the following methods to provide inputs:

- Selecting from a predefined list of text
- Voice dictation
- Selecting from a list of emojis

Getting Text Inputs

Getting text inputs from the Apple Watch is done through the `presentTextInput-ControllerWithSuggestions:allowedInputMode:completion:` method. This method presents an interface that can accept user inputs by showing the user a list of predefined texts, obtaining inputs through dictation, or selecting an emoji.

In the following exercise, you will learn how to obtain text (as well as emojis) from the user:

1. Using Xcode, create a new iOS App with WatchKit App project and name it **TextInputs**. Uncheck the option Include Notification Scene so that we can keep the WatchKit project to a bare minimum.

2. Select the Interface.storyboard file to edit it in the Storyboard Editor.

3. Drag and drop a Button control and a Label control onto the default Interface Controller (see Figure 4.46). Set the title of the button to **Select Symbol**, as shown.

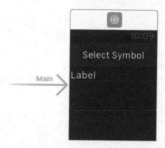

Figure 4.46   Adding the Button and Label
controls to the Interface Controller

4. Create an action for the button and name it **btnSelectSymbol**, and create
   an outlet for the Label control and name it **lblSymbolSelected** in the
   InterfaceController.swift file:

```swift
import WatchKit
import Foundation

class InterfaceController: WKInterfaceController {

    @IBOutlet var lblSymbolSelected: WKInterfaceLabel!

    @IBAction func btnSelectSymbol() {
    }
```

5. Add the following statements in bold to the InterfaceController.swift file:

```swift
import WatchKit
import Foundation

class InterfaceController: WKInterfaceController {

    @IBOutlet var lblSymbolSelected: WKInterfaceLabel!

    @IBAction func btnSelectSymbol() {
        presentTextInputControllerWithSuggestions(
            ["AAPL", "AMZN", "FB", "GOOG"],
            allowedInputMode: WKTextInputMode.Plain)
            { (results) -> Void in
            if results != nil {
                //---trying to see if the result can be converted to
                // String---
                if let symbol = results!.first as? String {
                    self.lblSymbolSelected.setText("Symbol: " + symbol)
```

```
                }
            }
        }
    }

    override func awakeWithContext(context: AnyObject?) {
        super.awakeWithContext(context)

        // Configure interface objects here.
        lblSymbolSelected.setText("")
    }
```

The `presentTextInputControllerWithSuggestions:allowedInputMode:`
`completion:` method takes in two arguments and a closure:

- An array of strings containing suggestions for the user to select.

- The input mode: plain text, emoji, or animated emoji.

- A block to execute after the user has dismissed the modal interface. The result is
  an optional array containing the input by the user. If the user has input a string
  or selected an emoji (see next section), the array contains a `String` object. If the
  user selects an animated emoji, the array contains an `NSData` object.

For this example, you ask the user to input plain text.

6. Select the WatchKit App scheme and run the project on the Apple Watch Simulator. Click **Select Symbol** on the Apple Watch Simulator (see Figure 4.47).
   You will be able to select from a list of predefined symbols. You can also tap the
   microphone button to use the Apple Watch's dictation capability to get text inputs.

Figure 4.47   Testing the application

Note

The Apple Watch Simulator does not support dictation.

Getting Emojis

As described in the previous section, the `presentTextInputControllerWith-Suggestions:allowedInputMode:completion:` method can also accept emojis or animated emojis. To get emojis, follow these steps:

1. Add an Image control to the Interface Controller in the Interface.storyboard file (see Figure 4.48).

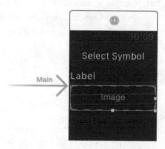

Figure 4.48   Adding an Image control
to the Interface Controller

2. Create an outlet for the Image control in the InterfaceController.swift file:

```
import WatchKit
import Foundation

class InterfaceController: WKInterfaceController {

    @IBOutlet var lblSymbolSelected: WKInterfaceLabel!
    @IBOutlet var image: WKInterfaceImage!
```

3. Add the following statements in bold to the InterfaceController.swift file:

```
import WatchKit
import Foundation

class InterfaceController: WKInterfaceController {

    @IBOutlet var lblSymbolSelected: WKInterfaceLabel!
    @IBOutlet var image: WKInterfaceImage!

    @IBAction func btnSelectSymbol() {
        presentTextInputControllerWithSuggestions(
            ["AAPL", "AMZN", "FB", "GOOG"],
            allowedInputMode: WKTextInputMode.AllowAnimatedEmoji)
```

```
{ (results) -> Void in
if results != nil {
    //---trying to see if the result can be converted to
    // String---
    if let symbol = results!.first as? String {
        self.lblSymbolSelected.setText("Symbol: " + symbol)
    } else {
        //---trying to see if the result can be converted to
        // NSData---
        if let emoji = results!.first as? NSData {
            //---display the animated emoji---
            self.image.setImageData(emoji)
        }
    }
}
}
}
```

In this example, you changed the input type to allow an animated emoji (`WKTextInputMode.AllowAnimatedEmoji`). When the user is done with the input, you try to typecast the first element of the result as a `String`. If this is successful, it means the user has entered (or selected) a text input or a nonanimated emoji. It not, you try to typecast the result as `NSData`, because it may contain an animated emoji. You can then display it using an Image control.

4. Select the WatchKit App scheme and run the project on the Apple Watch Simulator. Click **Select Symbol** on the Apple Watch Simulator. You will be able to select from a list of canned symbols. You can also click the emoji button (the button with the smiley; see Figure 4.49) to select from a list of emojis. You can swipe through four pages of emojis (the last page is nonanimated). An animated emoji that you have selected is displayed in the Image control, and a nonanimated emoji is shown in the Label control.

Figure 4.49   Users can select from a list of emojis

Laying Out the Controls

So far you have been using the various controls (e.g., Button, Table, Label) to display different types of information—text, images, etc. However, if you drag and drop the controls onto the Interface Controller, you will realize that most of the controls are displayed in a linear top-to-bottom layout. In this section, you learn how to group controls together using the Group control. The Group control is useful for acting as a container for other controls, and it can align the controls either vertically or horizontally. You can also nest Group controls.

1. Using Xcode, create a new iOS App with WatchKit App project and name it **Layouts**. Uncheck the option Include Notification Scene so that we can keep the WatchKit project to a bare minimum.
2. Select the Interface.storyboard file to edit it in the Storyboard Editor.
3. Add a Button control to the Interface Controller (see Figure 4.50).

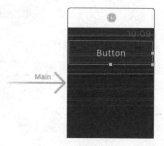

Figure 4.50   Adding a Button control
to the Interface Controller

4. Change the Title of the button to **1** and change its Width and Height to **40** (see Figure 4.51).
5. Copy and paste the button you modified in the previous step into the Interface Controller (see Figure 4.52) and change its title to **2**. Notice that the next button is displayed on the next line.

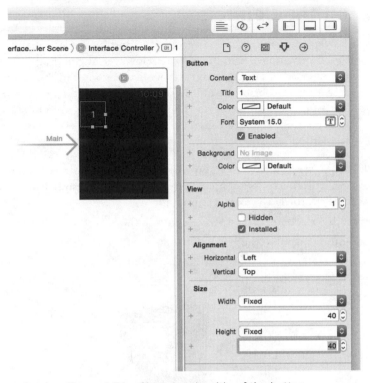

Figure 4.51   Changing the title of the button

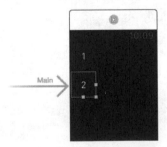

Figure 4.52   Duplicating the Button control

6. To group the two Button controls on the same line, you need to use a Group control. Drag and drop a Group control onto the Interface Controller as shown in Figure 4.53.

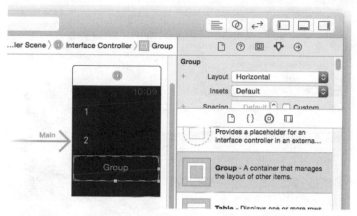

Figure 4.53   Adding a Group control to the Interface Controller

7. Drag and drop the two Button controls into the Group control one by one. The layout of the Interface Controller should now look like Figure 4.54.

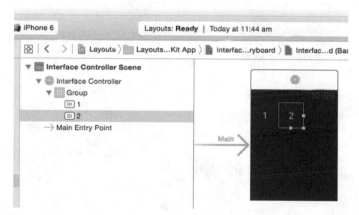

Figure 4.54   Moving the two Button controls into the Group control

8. Copy the button titled **2** and paste it into the Group control. Change its title to **3**. Then, copy the Group control and paste it onto the Interface Controller three times. Change the title of each button to **4, 5, 6, 7, 8, 9, ★, 0**, and **#**. The Interface Controller should now look like Figure 4.55.

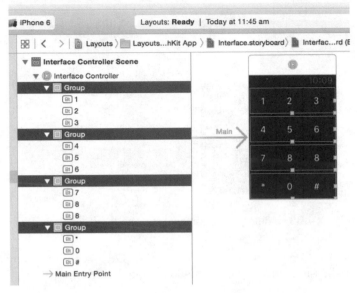

Figure 4.55   The Interface Controller now has four Group controls

9. Select the three Button controls in the first Group control and set their Horizontal position attributes to **Center** (see Figure 4.56).

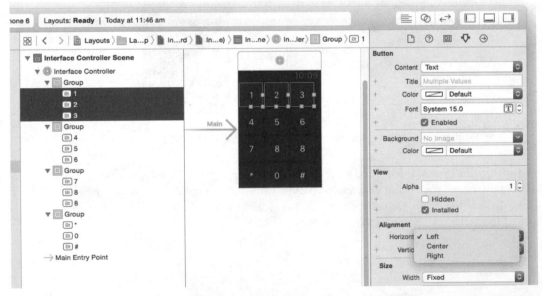

Figure 4.56   Centering the three Button controls

10. Repeat the previous step for the buttons in the next three Group controls.

11. Select the WatchKit App scheme and run the project on the Apple Watch Simulator. The Apple Watch Simulator should now display a nice number pad (see Figure 4.57).

Figure 4.57   The number pad containing 12 Button controls

For cases like this, it might be efficient to have a single action connected to the 12 Button controls. However, in WatchKit, unlike in UIKit (on the iPhone and iPad), the IBAction of each button does not contain a reference to the Button control initiating the touch:

```
@IBAction func btnClicked() {
}
```

Hence, you have to implement 12 different actions for the 12 buttons.

Force Touch

One of the unique features of the Apple Watch is Force Touch. Instead of tapping the various controls on the screen, you can press the screen with a small amount of force to bring up the context menu of the current Interface Controller.

Displaying a Context Menu

In this section, you learn how to use Force Touch to display a context menu for your Interface Controller:

1. Using Xcode, create a new iOS App with WatchKit App project and name it **ForceTouch**. Uncheck the option Include Notification Scene so that we can keep the WatchKit project to a bare minimum.

2. Select the Interface.storyboard file to edit it in the Storyboard Editor.

3. Add a Menu control to the Interface Controller (see Figure 4.58). Notice that the Menu control is not visible on the Interface Controller, and you can only see it in the hierarchical view.

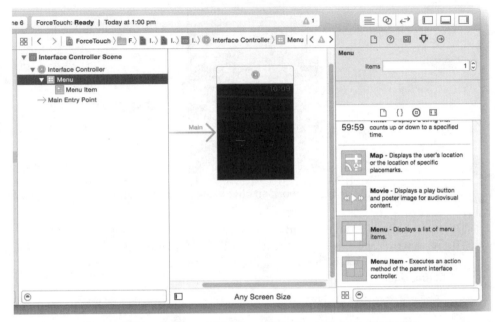

Figure 4.58   Adding a Menu control to the Interface Controller

4. Observe that the Menu control contains another control—Menu Item. Drag and drop another Menu Item control onto the Menu item as shown in Figure 4.59. The Menu control displays a context menu containing up to four menu items.

5. Drag and drop an image named Picture.png onto the Assets.xcassets file in the WatchKit App so that the Menu Item control can display an image (see Figure 4.60).

> **Note**
>
> The image to be displayed by the Menu Item control must be a template image. You can find a copy of the image used here in the source code download for this book.

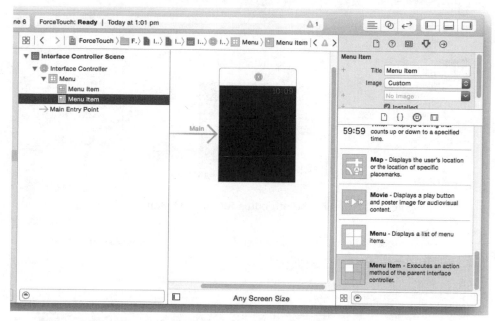

Figure 4.59   You can have up to four Menu Item controls in the Menu control

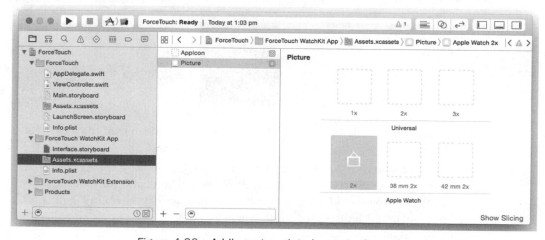

Figure 4.60   Adding a template image to the project

6. Select the first Menu Item control and set its Title to **Singapore** and its Image to **Custom | Picture** (see Figure 4.61).

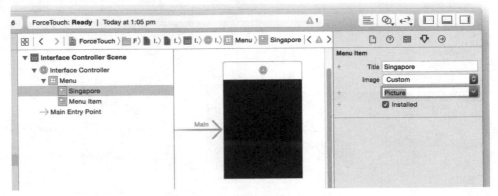

Figure 4.61   Setting the attributes for the first Menu Item control

7. Select the second Menu Item control and set its Title to **Norway** and its Image to
Custom | Picture (see Figure 4.62).

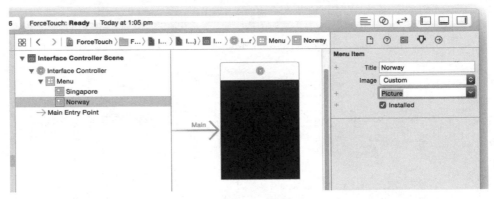

Figure 4.62   Setting the attributes for the second Menu Item control

8. Select the WatchKit App scheme and run the project on the Apple Watch Simulator. Press Command-Shift-2 on the Apple Watch Simulator (to simulate Force
Touch) and you should see the context menu displayed as shown in Figure 4.63.
Press Command-Shift-1 (to simulate single touch) and you can click either button
to dismiss the context menu.

9. Drag and drop two images named flag_norway.png and flag_singapore.png onto
the Assets.xcassets file in the WatchKit App as shown in Figure 4.64.

> **Note**
> You can find these two images in the source code download for this book.

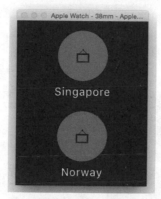

Figure 4.63   Displaying the context menu when you
long-click the Apple Watch Simulator

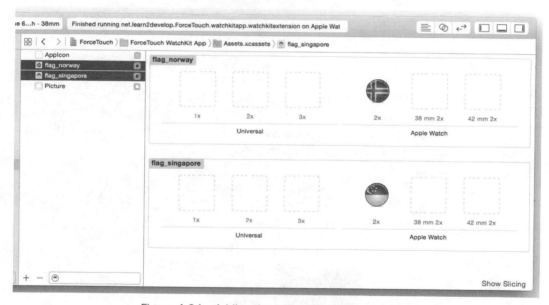

Figure 4.64   Adding the two images to the project

10. Drag and drop an Image control onto the Interface Controller and set its attributes
    (see Figure 4.65) as follows:

    Image: **flag_singapore**

    Horizontal: **Center**

    Vertical: **Center**

    Width: **Fixed | 60**

    Height: **Fixed | 60**

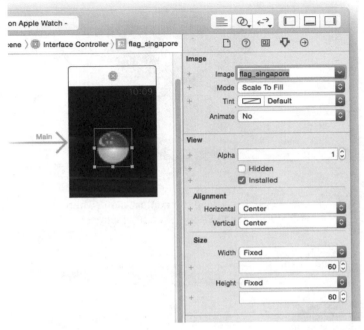

Figure 4.65   Adding an Image control to the Interface Controller

11. Drag and drop a Label control onto the Interface Controller and set the Text and Lines attributes as shown in Figure 4.66.

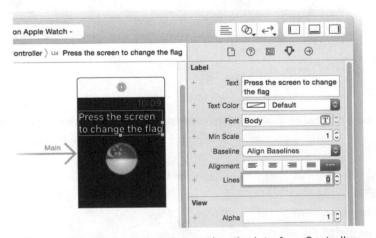

Figure 4.66   Adding a Label control to the Interface Controller

12. Using the **Show Assistant Editor** button, create an outlet for the Image control and two actions for each of the Menu Item controls in the InterfaceController .swift file. Add the code shown in bold:

```
import WatchKit
import Foundation

class InterfaceController: WKInterfaceController {

    @IBOutlet var image: WKInterfaceImage!

    @IBAction func mnuSingapore() {
        image.setImageNamed("flag_singapore")
    }

    @IBAction func mnuNorway() {
        image.setImageNamed("flag_norway")
    }
```

13. Select the WatchKit App scheme and run the project on the Apple Watch Simulator. Long-click the Apple Watch Simulator and you should see the context menu. Selecting either button sets the Image control to display the flag for the respective country (see Figure 4.67).

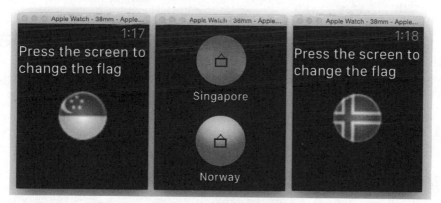

Figure 4.67   Changing the flag by selecting the country in the context menu

Adding Menu Items Programmatically

Instead of adding Menu Item controls to a Menu control during design time, sometimes a situation dictates that you add the Menu Item controls programmatically during runtime:

1. Using the same project used in the previous section, add the following statements in bold to the InterfaceController.swift file:

```
import WatchKit
import Foundation
```

```
class InterfaceController: WKInterfaceController {

    @IBOutlet var image: WKInterfaceImage!
    @IBAction func mnuSingapore() {
        image.setImageNamed("flag_singapore")
    }

    @IBAction func mnuNorway() {
        image.setImageNamed("flag_norway")
    }

    func mnuCancel() {
        //---user tapped Cancel---
    }

    override func awakeWithContext(context: AnyObject?) {
        super.awakeWithContext(context)

        // Configure interface objects here.
        self.addMenuItemWithItemIcon(
            WKMenuItemIcon.Decline,
            title: "Cancel",
            action: "mnuCancel")
    }
```

These statements programmatically add a Menu Item control to the Interface Controller and set its image using one of the built-in icons—Decline. It also sets its title to **Cancel** and assigns its action to the mnuCancel function.

2. Select the WatchKit App scheme and run the project on the Apple Watch Simulator. When you long-click the Apple Watch Simulator, you should see the context menu as shown in Figure 4.68.

Figure 4.68   The context menu with the third button

3. If you want to set the image to your own, use the `addMenuItemWithImage-Named:title:action:` method.

Summary

In this chapter, you looked at the various controls that you can use to display and gather information in your Apple Watch application. You also looked at how to use Force Touch to display a context menu in your application. In the next chapter, you look at additional controls, such as Date and Map, as well as how to interact with the containing iOS application to develop really cool Apple Watch applications!

5

Accessing the Apple Watch Hardware

This is what customers pay us for—to sweat all these details so it's easy and pleasant for them to use our computers. We're supposed to be really good at this. That doesn't mean we don't listen to customers, but it's hard for them to tell you what they want when they've never seen anything remotely like it.

Steve Jobs

In watchOS 1.0, Apple did not provide third-party developers access to the various hardware features of the Apple Watch, such as the accelerometer, microphone, and Taptic Engine. However, in watchOS 2, Apple has exposed some of these features to developers so that they can create more exciting watch apps.

In this chapter, you learn how to access some of these hardware features and see how they can be useful to the apps you are building.

Making Phone Calls and Sending Messages

In watchOS 2, your watch app can now directly make a phone call or send a message. To do so, follow these steps:

1. Using Xcode, create a new iOS App with WatchKit App project and name it **NewCapabilities**. Uncheck the option Include Notification Scene so that we can keep the WatchKit project to a bare minimum.

2. Select the Interface.storyboard file to edit it in the Storyboard Editor.

3. Drag and drop two Button controls onto the Interface Controller, as shown in Figure 5.1.

Figure 5.1   Populating the Interface Controller

4. Create two actions for the buttons in the InterfaceController.swift file:

```
import WatchKit
import Foundation

class InterfaceController: WKInterfaceController {

    @IBAction func btnCallPhone() {
    }
    @IBAction func btnSendMessage() {
    }
```

5. Add the following statements in bold to the InterfaceController.swift file:

```
import WatchKit
import Foundation

class InterfaceController: WKInterfaceController {

    @IBAction func btnCallPhone() {
        if let url = NSURL(string: "tel:1234567") {
            WKExtension.sharedExtension().openSystemURL(url)
        }
    }

    @IBAction func btnSendMessage() {
        if let url = NSURL(string: "sms:1234567") {
            WKExtension.sharedExtension().openSystemURL(url)
        }
    }
```

The `sharedExtension` method of the `WKExtension` class returns a copy of the WatchKit Extension object, which you can use to open URLs. The `openSystemURL:` method allows you to launch another application using a URL scheme. In the current version of WatchKit, only the `tel:` (for making a phone call) and `sms:` (for sending messages) schemes are supported.

6. Select the WatchKit App scheme and run the project on a real Apple Watch. Tapping the **Call Phone** button (Figure 5.2, left) directly places a phone call on the iPhone (see Figure 5.2, middle), and tapping **Send Message** allows you to compose a message (see Figure 5.2, right) and send it through the iPhone's Messages app.

Figure 5.2   Making a phone call and sending messages directly from the Apple Watch

Recording Audio

The Apple Watch has a built-in microphone that allows you to make dictation and place phone calls. In watchOS 2, your apps have access to the microphone to perform audio recordings:

1. Using Xcode, create a new iOS App with WatchKit App project and name it **AudioRecord**. Uncheck the option Include Notification Scene so that we can keep the WatchKit project to a bare minimum.
2. Select the Interface.storyboard file to edit it in the Storyboard Editor.
3. Drag and drop a Button control onto the Interface Controller and set its title to **Record Audio**, as shown in Figure 5.3.

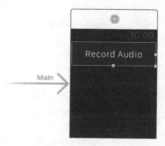

Figure 5.3   Populating the Interface Controller

4. Create an action for the button in the InterfaceController.swift file:

```
import WatchKit
import Foundation

class InterfaceController: WKInterfaceController {

    @IBAction func btnRecordAudio() {
    }
```

5. Add the following statements in bold to the InterfaceController.swift file:

```
import WatchKit
import Foundation

class InterfaceController: WKInterfaceController {
    var filePath:NSURL!
    @IBAction func btnRecordAudio() {
        if let dir : NSString = NSSearchPathForDirectoriesInDomains(
            NSSearchPathDirectory.DocumentDirectory,
            NSSearchPathDomainMask.AllDomainsMask, true).first {
                //---format can be wav, mp4, or m4a---
                let path = dir.stringByAppendingPathComponent(
                    "myrecording.wav");
                filePath = NSURL(string: path)
                let audioOptions = [
                    WKAudioRecorderControllerOptionsActionTitleKey:
                        "Save",
            WKAudioRecorderControllerOptionsAlwaysShowActionTitleKey:
                true,
                    WKAudioRecorderControllerOptionsAutorecordKey:true,
                WKAudioRecorderControllerOptionsMaximumDurationKey:5.0
                ]
                presentAudioRecorderControllerWithOutputURL(filePath!,
                    preset: WKAudioRecorderPreset.HighQualityAudio,
                    options: audioOptions as [NSObject : AnyObject],
                    completion: {
                    (didSave, error) -> Void in
                    if didSave {
                        print("Audio saved!")
                        let options =
                            [WKMediaPlayerControllerOptionsAutoplayKey:
                                true]
                        self.presentMediaPlayerControllerWithURL(
                            self.filePath, options: options) {
                            (didPlayToEnd, endTime, error) -> Void in
                            if didPlayToEnd {
                                print("Movie finished playback")
                            }
```

```
                    if error != nil {
                        print(error!.description)
                    }
                }
            }
            if error != nil {
                print(error!.description)
            }
        })
    }
}
```

In the previous statements, you first created a path to save the audio recording. In particular, you saved it into the Documents directory on the Apple Watch. You then created a dictionary containing the various options to record the audio:

- WKAudioRecorderControllerOptionsActionTitleKey specifies the title to display (in the top-right corner) when the Audio Recorder Controller is displayed.

- WKAudioRecorderControllerOptionsAlwaysShowActionTitleKey specifies whether to show the title on the Audio Recorder Controller.

- WKAudioRecorderControllerOptionsAutorecordKey specifies if audio recording should commence automatically when the Audio Recorder Controller is shown.

- WKAudioRecorderControllerOptionsMaximumDurationKey specifies the maximum duration of the audio recording in seconds. To indicate no maximum duration, use NSTimeInterval.infinity.

To display the Audio Recorder Controller, call the presentAudioRecorderControllerWithOutputURL:preset:options:completion: method. This method takes in the following arguments:

- The quality of the audio to record, which could be HighQualityAudio, NarrowBandSpeech, or WideBandSpeech

- The options dictionary as just described

- A completion handler indicating if the audio recording is saved successfully and any errors

Once the audio is recorded, you can play it back using the presentMediaPlayerControllerWithURL:options: method.

6. Select the WatchKit App scheme and run the project on a real Apple Watch. When you tap the **Record Audio** button, you are prompted to give permission to access the microphone on the Apple Watch (see Figure 5.4). You are also prompted for permission on your iPhone.

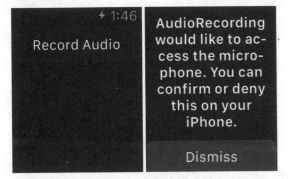

Figure 5.4   Running the app for the first time requires granting permission to the app to use the microphone on the watch

7. Once permission is given, tap the **Record Audio** button again. This time, you should see the Audio Recorder (see Figure 5.5). As you have specified the recording to start automatically, the recording starts immediately and records for five seconds (also specified by you). Once the recording is done, you can tap the **Save** button to save the audio recording (the controller will close thereafter), or tap the **Play** button to review what you have just recorded.

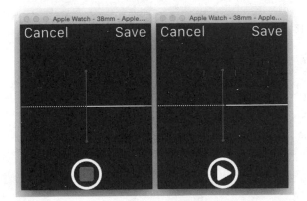

Figure 5.5   Audio recording in action

Digital Crown

In the current release of WatchKit for watchOS 2, Apple allows only the following uses of the Digital Crown:

- Scrolling page content in third-party apps. This basically means that if your Interface Controller has more controls than the screen of the Apple Watch can display, turning the Digital Crown allows you to scroll the page up and down, revealing the controls.

- The new Picker control in watchOS 2 allows users to select an item by turning the Digital Crown. The Picker control is discussed in Chapter 4, "Displaying and Gathering Information."

At the moment, third-party developers are not allowed to register custom event handlers for the Digital Crown. This feature would interest a lot of developers and will likely be available in a future release of the WatchKit.

Accelerometer

The Apple Watch comes with a multitude of sensors. One of them, the accelerometer, is available to third-party developers in watchOS 2. Using the accelerometer, you can measure the acceleration experienced by the Apple Watch in three axes: x-axis, y-axis, and z-axis. With this data, you can build applications that measure the activity level of your users.

1. Using Xcode, create a new iOS App with WatchKit App project and name it **UsingCoreMotion**. Uncheck the option Include Notification Scene so that we can keep the WatchKit project to a bare minimum.
2. Select the Interface.storyboard file to edit it in the Storyboard Editor.
3. Drag and drop three Label controls onto the Interface Controller, as shown in Figure 5.6.

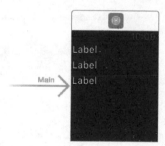

Figure 5.6   Populating the Interface Controller

4. Create three outlets for the labels in the InterfaceController.swift file:

```
import WatchKit
import Foundation

class InterfaceController: WKInterfaceController {
    @IBOutlet var labelX: WKInterfaceLabel!
    @IBOutlet var labelY: WKInterfaceLabel!
    @IBOutlet var labelZ: WKInterfaceLabel!
```

5. Add the following statements in bold to the InterfaceController.swift file:

```swift
import WatchKit
import Foundation
import CoreMotion

class InterfaceController: WKInterfaceController {
    var motionManager: CMMotionManager!

    @IBOutlet var labelX: WKInterfaceLabel!
    @IBOutlet var labelY: WKInterfaceLabel!
    @IBOutlet var labelZ: WKInterfaceLabel!

    override func awakeWithContext(context: AnyObject?) {
        super.awakeWithContext(context)

        // Configure interface objects here.
        motionManager = CMMotionManager()
        motionManager.accelerometerUpdateInterval = 0.1

        print(
            "Accelerometer: \(motionManager.accelerometerAvailable)")
        print(
            "Gyroscope: \(motionManager.gyroAvailable)")
        print(
            "Magnetometer: \(motionManager.magnetometerAvailable)")
        print(
            "Device Motion: \(motionManager.deviceMotionAvailable)")
    }

    override func willActivate() {
        // This method is called when watch view controller is about
        // to be visible to user.
        super.willActivate()

        let handler:CMAccelerometerHandler =
        {
            (data: CMAccelerometerData?, error: NSError?) -> Void in
            self.labelX.setText(
                String(format: "x - %.2f", data!.acceleration.x))
            self.labelY.setText(
                String(format: "y - %.2f", data!.acceleration.y))
            self.labelZ.setText(
                String(format: "z - %.2f", data!.acceleration.z))
        }
        motionManager.startAccelerometerUpdatesToQueue(
            NSOperationQueue.currentQueue()!,
            withHandler: handler)
```

```
        print("Start updating...")
    }


    override func didDeactivate() {
        // This method is called when watch view controller is no
        // longer visible.
        super.didDeactivate()

        motionManager.stopAccelerometerUpdates()
        print("Stop updating...")
    }
}
```

With these statements,

- You created an instance of the CMMotionManager class. The CMMotionManager class provides a range of motion services provided by iOS and watchOS. While the CMMotionManager class on iOS provides data from services, such as the accelerometer, gyroscope, magnetometer, and device motion, only the accelerometer data is exposed by the CMMotionManager class in watchOS 2. You can verify this by checking the various properties of the CMMotionManager object, such as accelerometerAvailable, gyroAvailable, and so on.

- You created a handler block of type CMAccelerometerHandler, which takes in two parameters—accelerometer data of type CMAccelerometerData, and an optional error of type NSError. The accelerometer data consists of the acceleration experienced by the Apple Watch in the three axes: x, y, and z. To get data from the accelerometer, use the startAccelerometerUpdates-ToQueue:withHandler: method of the CMMotionManager object, which takes in an NSOperationQueue object and a handler block to handle new accelerometer data. As the accelerometer data might come in at a high rate, you should not pass in the main operation queue. Instead, you should use the current operation queue.

To stop the accelerometer, call the stopAccelerometerUpdates method of the CMMotionManager object.

6. Select the WatchKit App scheme and run the project on a real Apple Watch. Observe the data displayed on the Apple Watch (see Figure 5.7). You should also see the following in the Output window:

Accelerometer: true

Gyroscope: false

Magnetometer: false

Device Motion: false

Figure 5.7   Viewing the accelerometer data

Taptic Engine

The Apple Watch has a built-in vibrator, known as the Taptic Engine. This little device produces haptic feedback. Coupled with audio cues, the Taptic Engine provides an enhanced user experience. Some of the controls in the WatchKit already support the Taptic Engine. For example, both the Table and Picker controls produce haptic feedback when the user scrolls beyond the first or last item in the control.

In watchOS 2, developers can now access the Taptic Engine directly in their code. The following example shows how:

1. Using Xcode, create a new iOS App with WatchKit App project and name it **TapticEngine**. Uncheck the option Include Notification Scene so that we can keep the WatchKit project to a bare minimum.

2. Select the Interface.storyboard file to edit it in the Storyboard Editor.

3. Drag and drop a Picker and a Button control (set its title to **Tap Me!**) onto the Interface Controller, as shown in Figure 5.8.

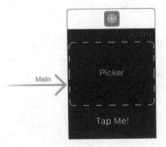

Figure 5.8   Populating the Interface Controller

4. Create an outlet and an action for the Picker control and an action for the Button control in the InterfaceController.swift file:

```swift
import WatchKit
import Foundation

class InterfaceController: WKInterfaceController {
    @IBOutlet var picker: WKInterfacePicker!

    @IBAction func pickerChanged(value: Int) {
    }

    @IBAction func btnTapMe() {
    }
```

5. Add the following statements in bold to the InterfaceController.swift file:

```swift
import WatchKit
import Foundation

class InterfaceController: WKInterfaceController {
    @IBOutlet var picker: WKInterfacePicker!

    var selectedHapticType = 0

    //---an array containing the haptic types---
    let hapticTypes = [
        "Notification",
        "DirectionUp",
        "DirectionDown",
        "Success",
        "Failure",
        "Retry",
        "Start",
        "Stop",
        "Click"
    ]
    @IBAction func btnTapMe() {
        WKInterfaceDevice.currentDevice().playHaptic(
            WKHapticType(rawValue: selectedHapticType)!)
    }

    @IBAction func pickerChanged(value: Int) {
        selectedHapticType = value
    }
```

```
override func awakeWithContext(context: AnyObject?) {
    super.awakeWithContext(context)

    //---an array of WKPickItems---
    var items = [WKPickerItem]()
    for hapticType in hapticTypes {
        let item = WKPickerItem()
        item.title = hapticType
        items.append(item)
    }
    //---populate the Picker with the list of haptic types---
    picker.setItems(items)
}
```

In the previous code, you first created an array of haptic types supported by the Taptic Engine. You then used the Picker control to list all these haptic types so that the user can select one of them and try it out. When the user taps on the **Tap Me!** button, you use the `playHaptic:` method of the `WKInterfaceDevice` instance to play the selected haptic.

6. Select the WatchKit App scheme and run the project on a real Apple Watch. Select a haptic type on the Apple Watch (see Figure 5.9) and tap the **Tap Me!** button. You should be able to feel the watch vibrating and hear the accompanying audio cue.

Figure 5.9   Trying out the Taptic Engine

Summary

In this chapter, you saw that watchOS 2 exposes several APIs for you to access the various hardware on the Apple Watch. Although not all the hardware features are exposed, this represents a good way for you to start integrating additional features into your Apple Watch apps.

6

Programming Complications

Sometimes when you innovate, you make mistakes.
It is best to admit them quickly, and get on with
improving your other innovations.

Steve Jobs

Complications on watches have always been one of the key differentiators of expensive timepieces. Put simply, a *complication* is a function on a timepiece that does more than just tell the time. Complications on a timepiece include alarms, tachymeters, chronographs, calendars, and so on. Figure 6.1 shows an example of complications on a watch.

Figure 6.1   A watch with multiple complications

Apple has also aptly implemented complications on its various Apple Watch faces; numerous watch faces contain complications that display data from applications like Activity, Calendar, Weather, and so on. Figure 6.2 shows a watch face on the Apple Watch displaying five complications.

Figure 6.2   A watch face on the Apple Watch with five complications

In watchOS 2, third-party apps can now also display data in watch face complications. In this chapter, I walk you through the process of creating an application that displays complication data.

Introducing the ClockKit Framework

The *ClockKit Framework* manages all the data displayed by the complications on the watch face on an Apple Watch. To support complications in your watch app, you need to provide a complication data source so that ClockKit can use the data for displaying on the watch face. Specifically, you need to implement the `CLKComplicationDataSource` protocol. This protocol contains the following methods:

- `getSupportedTimeTravelDirectionsForComplication:withHandler:` is called to retrieve the Time Travel directions that your complication supports.

- `getTimelineStartDateForComplication:withHandler:` is called to retrieve the earliest date that your complication is ready to supply data.

- `getTimelineEndDateForComplication:withHandler:` is called to retrieve the latest date that your complication is ready to supply data.

- `getPrivacyBehaviorForComplication:withHandler:` returns the privacy behavior for the specified complication style.

- `getCurrentTimelineEntryForComplication:withHandler:` is called to display the timeline entry you want to display now.

- `getTimelineEntriesForComplication:beforeDate:limit:withHandler:` is called to retrieve past timeline entries for the complication.

- `getTimelineEntriesForComplication:afterDate:limit:withHandler:` is called to retrieve future timeline entries for the complication.

- `getNextRequestedUpdateDateWithHandler:` is called to get the next update time for the complication.

- `getPlaceholderTemplateForComplication:withHandler:` returns a static template to display in the selection screen for your complication.

The ClockKit Framework executes all the methods in the background well before the watch face displays your data in the complications. This execution model allows the user to instantly see the data displayed in the complications when the watch face lights up (such as when the user raises his or her wrist). Also, this gives the ClockKit Framework class sufficient time to fetch the data to be displayed in the complications.

> **Note**
>
> Time Travel is a new feature in watchOS 2 that allows your application to display time-sensitive information on watch faces with complications. Turning the Digital Crown back and forth displays events past and future. You learn more about this in the "Time Travel" section later in this chapter.

Placement for Complications

Complications on the Apple Watch are classified into the following families (see Figure 6.3):

- **Modular Small**: A medium-size square area used in digital interfaces
- **Modular Large**: A large rectangular area used in digital interfaces
- **Utilitarian Small**: A small square or rectangular area used in analog interfaces
- **Utilitarian Large**: A rectangular area that spans the width of the screen used in analog interfaces
- **Circular Small**: A small circular area used in analog interfaces

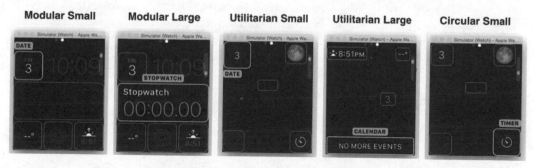

Figure 6.3   The various complication families

Note that the first two families (Modular Small and Modular Large) are used in digital watch faces, while the rest are used in analog watch faces.

The types of complications available are dependent on the individual watch faces; some watch faces support multiple complication families, while some do not support complications at all.

Using the Template Classes

For each of the complication families, you can use a complication template class to display the data in the complication. Table 6.1 shows the list of complication template classes that you can use for each complication family.

Table 6.1   Complication Templates for Each Complication Family

Complication Families	Complication Templates
Modular Small	CLKComplicationTemplateModularSmallColumnsText
	CLKComplicationTemplateModularSmallRingImage
	CLKComplicationTemplateModularSmallRingText
	CLKComplicationTemplateModularSmallSimpleImage
	CLKComplicationTemplateModularSmallSimpleText
	CLKComplicationTemplateModularSmallStackImage
	CLKComplicationTemplateModularSmallStackText
Modular Large	CLKComplicationTemplateModularLargeColumns
	CLKComplicationTemplateModularLargeStandardBody
	CLKComplicationTemplateModularLargeTable
	CLKComplicationTemplateModularLargeTallBody
Circular Small	CLKComplicationTemplateCircularSmallRingImage
	CLKComplicationTemplateCircularSmallRingText
	CLKComplicationTemplateCircularSmallSimpleImage
	CLKComplicationTemplateCircularSmallSimpleText
	CLKComplicationTemplateCircularSmallStackImage
	CLKComplicationTemplateCircularSmallStackText
Utilitarian Small	CLKComplicationTemplateUtilitarianSmallFlat
	CLKComplicationTemplateUtilitarianSmallRingImage
	CLKComplicationTemplateUtilitarianSmallRingText
	CLKComplicationTemplateUtilitarianSmallSquare
Utilitarian Large	CLKComplicationTemplateUtilitarianLargeFlat

You learn how to use some of these template classes in the next section.

Building a Movie Showtime Complication Example

Now that you have a better idea of complications on the Apple Watch, let's create a project to display complication data on the watch face.

In this project, your application displays information about movies that are currently playing in a theater. You display information on two complications:

- The timing of the various movies playing in a theater, past and present
- The rating of each movie

Creating the Project

To create the project, follow these steps:

1. Using Xcode, create an iOS App with WatchKit App project (see Figure 6.4).

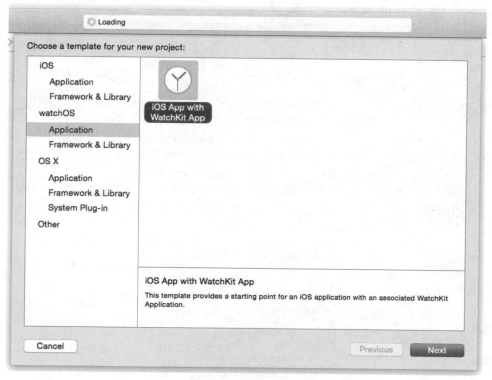

Figure 6.4   Creating a WatchKit App project

2. Name the project **Movies**. Also, uncheck the Include Notification Scene option and check the Include Complication option (see Figure 6.5). This makes Xcode configure the project with complication support.

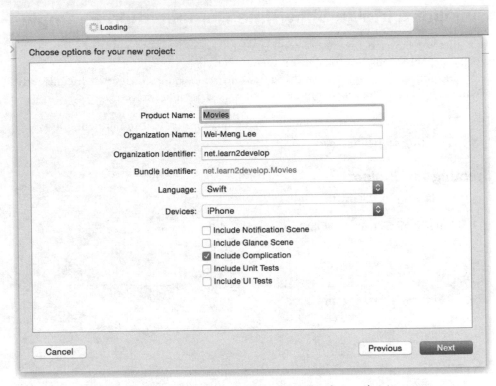

Figure 6.5   Check the Include Complication option to
support complications in your application

3. When the project is created, observe that under Movies WatchKit Extension you
have a file named ComplicationController.swift (see Figure 6.6).

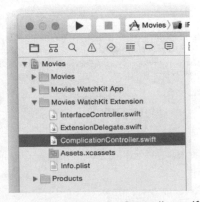

Figure 6.6   The ComplicationController.swift file is
used for displaying complication data

The ComplicationController.swift file contains the definition for the ComplicationController class, which implements the CLKComplication-DataSource protocol (described earlier in the "Introducing the ClockKit Framework" section). This protocol allows you to implement all the methods that pass your complication data to the ClockKit Framework.

Selecting Complication Families Support

In the Project Navigator, selecting the Movies WatchKit Extension target shows all the complication families supported by your app (see Figure 6.7). You can uncheck those that you do not want to support. For this example, leave them all selected.

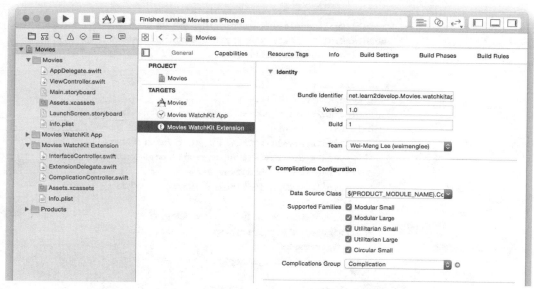

Figure 6.7   You can select which complication families your application supports

Creating the Complication Placeholder Template

Let's now implement the first method in the ComplicationController class: getPlaceholderTemplateForComplication:withHandler:. This method returns a static template to display in the selection screen for your complication.

1. Add the following statements in bold to the ComplicationController.swift file:

```
import ClockKit


//---multipliers to convert to seconds---
let HOUR: NSTimeInterval = 60 * 60
let MINUTE: NSTimeInterval = 60
```

```
func getPlaceholderTemplateForComplication(
    complication: CLKComplication,
    withHandler handler: (CLKComplicationTemplate?) -> Void) {
    // This method will be called once per supported complication, and
    // the results will be cached.

    // handler(nil)
    var template: CLKComplicationTemplate?
    switch complication.family {
    case .ModularSmall:
        let modularSmallTemplate =
            CLKComplicationTemplateModularSmallRingText()
        modularSmallTemplate.textProvider =
            CLKSimpleTextProvider(text: "R")
        modularSmallTemplate.fillFraction = 0.75
        modularSmallTemplate.ringStyle = CLKComplicationRingStyle.Closed
        template = modularSmallTemplate

    case .ModularLarge:
        let modularLargeTemplate =
            CLKComplicationTemplateModularLargeStandardBody()
        modularLargeTemplate.headerTextProvider =
            CLKTimeIntervalTextProvider(startDate: NSDate(),
                endDate: NSDate(timeIntervalSinceNow: 1.5 * HOUR))
        modularLargeTemplate.body1TextProvider =
            CLKSimpleTextProvider(text: "Movie Name",
                shortText: "Movie")
        modularLargeTemplate.body2TextProvider =
            CLKSimpleTextProvider(text: "Running Time",
                shortText: "Time")
        template = modularLargeTemplate

    case .UtilitarianSmall:
        template = nil

    case .UtilitarianLarge:
        template = nil

    case .CircularSmall:
        template = nil
    }
    handler(template)
}
```

In this method, you first check which types of complications you want to support by examining the CLKComplication object that is passed in. For simplicity, in this chapter the code supports both the Modular Small and Modular Large complications. Once you determine the types of complications you want to support, you need to use one of the many templates available for each complication:

- For the Modular Small complication, use the `CLKComplicationTemplate-ModularSmallRingText` class. This class allows you to display a single text string encircled by a configurable progress ring.

- For the Modular Large complication, use the `CLKComplicationTemplate-ModularLargeStandardBody` class. This class displays a header row with two lines of text.

- For the rest of complications that you are not supporting, simply pass `nil` to the `handler` method.

> **Note**
>
> To display a string in a complication, you do not use the usual `NSString` class. Instead, you use the `CLKSimpleTextProvider` class. This class displays a single line of text. It also contains an abbreviated version of the string so that in cases where the string is too long to be displayed, it first uses the abbreviated version of the string before truncating it.
>
> Besides the `CLKSimpleTextProvider` class, you also use the `CLKTimeIntervalTextProvider` class to display a string that shows a range of time. This class is smart enough to display the string efficiently by taking into consideration the space available for display and the user's region and locale.

2. To test the application, select the **Complication – Movies WatchKit App** scheme at the top of Xcode (see Figure 6.8), and then select **iPhone 6 + Apple Watch – 38mm**. Press Command-R to deploy the applications onto the simulators.

Figure 6.8   Selecting the complication scheme in Xcode

This deploys the iOS app and the WatchKit app onto the iPhone 6 and Apple Watch Simulator, respectively.

3. On the Apple Watch Simulator, press Command-Shift-2 to simulate a deep press. Then, click the watch face. You see that you can now customize the watch face, as shown in Figure 6.9.

Figure 6.9   Customizing the watch face

4. Press Command–Shift–1 to simulate a shallow press. Then, swipe the watch face to the left. You should now see the **MODULAR** watch face, as shown in Figure 6.10.

Figure 6.10   Changing to the **MODULAR** watch face

5. Click **Customize**. You now see that you can customize the watch face (see Figure 6.11).

6. Click and swipe to the left and you should see the watch face as shown in Figure 6.12.

7. Select the complication of the watch face named **CALENDAR** and move the scroll wheel on your mouse (or move two fingers on the trackpad). The complication changes. Move the scroll wheel until you reach the **MOVIES WATCHKIT APP** item (the name of your app; see Figure 6.13).

Figure 6.11   Customizing the watch face

Figure 6.12   Changing to the next customizable
screen of the watch face

Figure 6.13 Changing the complication to
your project (Modular Large)

8. Select the complication in the middle of the bottom row (the one that says **ACTIVITY**; see Figure 6.14).

Figure 6.14   Selecting the next complication to change

9. Move the scroll wheel (or two fingers on the trackpad) until you see **MOVIES WATCHKIT APP** (see Figure 6.15).

Figure 6.15   Changing the complication
to your project (Modular Small)

10. Press Command-Shift-2 and then click the watch face (see Figure 6.16).

11. Press Command-Shift-1 and click the watch face. The watch face should now look like Figure 6.17.

Figure 6.16 Deep-pressing the watch face
to exit the customization mode

Figure 6.17 The watch face with
complication data from your app

The first complication displays the following:

- A header showing a time interval of 1.5 hours, starting from the time the complication was added
- Two lines of text: "Movie Name" and "Running Time"

The second complication displays a three-quarters–complete circle, with the letter *R* within it.

Setting Privacy Behavior

The next method you need to implement is the `getPrivacyBehaviorFor-Complication:withHandler:` method, which returns the privacy behavior for the specified complication style.

If you want the complication data to display even if the watch is locked, use the ShowOnLockScreen enumeration:

```
func getPrivacyBehaviorForComplication(
    complication: CLKComplication,
    withHandler handler: (CLKComplicationPrivacyBehavior) -> Void) {
    handler(.ShowOnLockScreen)
}
```

If not, use the HideOnLockScreen enumeration.

Populating the Complications with Real Data

Now that you can display the template complication, let's display some real data so that you can see how complications really work:

1. In the ComplicationController.swift file (from the Movies project created in the previous section), add the following statements in bold:

```
import ClockKit

//---multipliers to convert to seconds---
let HOUR: NSTimeInterval = 60 * 60
let MINUTE: NSTimeInterval = 60

struct Movie {
    var movieName: String
    var runningTime: NSTimeInterval  //---in seconds---
    var runningDate: NSDate
    var rating:Float                  //---1 to 10---
}

class ComplicationController: NSObject, CLKComplicationDataSource {

    //---in real life, the movies can be loaded from a web service or file
    // system---
    let movies = [
        Movie(movieName: "Terminator 2: Judgment Day",
            runningTime: 137 * MINUTE,
            runningDate: NSDate(timeIntervalSinceNow: -360 * MINUTE),
            rating:8),
        Movie(movieName: "World War Z",
            runningTime: 116 * MINUTE,
            runningDate: NSDate(timeIntervalSinceNow: -120 * MINUTE),
            rating:7),
        Movie(movieName: "Secondhand Lions",
            runningTime: 90 * MINUTE,
            runningDate: NSDate(timeIntervalSinceNow: 10 * MINUTE),
            rating:8),
```

```
Movie(movieName: "The Dark Knight",
    runningTime: 152 * MINUTE,
    runningDate: NSDate(timeIntervalSinceNow: 120 * MINUTE),
    rating:9),
Movie(movieName: "The Prestige",
    runningTime: 130 * MINUTE,
    runningDate: NSDate(timeIntervalSinceNow: 360 * MINUTE),
    rating:8),
]
```

The previous statements created a structure to store movie information, and the movies array stored a list of Movie instances. Figure 6.18 shows the timeline of each movie and its corresponding showtime.

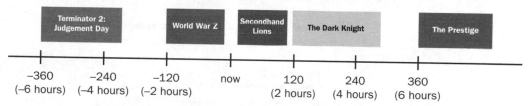

Figure 6.18   Visualization of the timelines of the various movies

> **Note**
>
> I have programmatically set the timeline of each movie with respect to the current time so that it is easier for you to test your application. In real life, the content of the movies array would be fetched dynamically from a web service or the file system of the iPhone.

2. The next method to implement is the getCurrentTimelineEntryFor-Complication:withHandler: method. This method is called to display the timeline entry you want to display now. Add the following statements in bold to the ComplicationController.swift file:

```
func getCurrentTimelineEntryForComplication(
    complication: CLKComplication,
    withHandler handler: ((CLKComplicationTimelineEntry?) -> Void)) {
    // Call the handler with the current timeline entry.

    // handler(nil)
    for movie in movies {
        //---display the movie that is currently playing or the next one
        // that is coming up---
        if (movie.runningDate.timeIntervalSinceNow) >= 0) {
```

```
switch complication.family {
case .ModularSmall:
    let modularSmallTemplate =
        CLKComplicationTemplateModularSmallRingText()

    modularSmallTemplate.textProvider =
        CLKSimpleTextProvider(text: "\(Int(movie.rating))")

    modularSmallTemplate.fillFraction = movie.rating / 10

    modularSmallTemplate.ringStyle =
        CLKComplicationRingStyle.Closed

    let entry = CLKComplicationTimelineEntry(
        date:NSDate(),
        complicationTemplate: modularSmallTemplate)
    handler(entry)

case .ModularLarge:
    let modularLargeTemplate =
        CLKComplicationTemplateModularLargeStandardBody()

    modularLargeTemplate.headerTextProvider =
        CLKTimeIntervalTextProvider(
            startDate: movie.runningDate,
            endDate: NSDate(
                timeInterval: movie.runningTime,
                sinceDate: movie.runningDate))

    modularLargeTemplate.body1TextProvider =
        CLKSimpleTextProvider(
            text: movie.movieName,
            shortText: movie.movieName)

    modularLargeTemplate.body2TextProvider =
        CLKSimpleTextProvider(
            text: "\(movie.runningTime / MINUTE) mins",
            shortText: nil)

    let entry = CLKComplicationTimelineEntry(
        date:NSDate(),
        complicationTemplate: modularLargeTemplate)

    handler(entry)

case .UtilitarianSmall:
    handler(nil)
```

```
        case .UtilitarianLarge:
            handler(nil)

        case .CircularSmall:
            handler(nil)
        }
    }
}
```

When the `getCurrentTimelineEntryForComplication:withHandler:`
method is fired, you want to display the next upcoming movie. So, you iterate through
each movie and check to see if the difference between the movie's running time and the
current time is more than or equal to 0 (movies that started playing before the current
time have a negative value for the `timeIntervalSinceNow` property):

```
for movie in movies {
    //---display the movie that is currently playing or the next one
    // that is coming up---
    if (movie.runningDate.timeIntervalSinceNow >= 0) {
```

Once the first movie is located, you create a `CLKComplicationTimelineEntry`
object to display the complication.

Note

A `CLKComplicationTimelineEntry` object represents the complication data
to display at a specific date. You use a timeline entry to specify the date at which to
display a specific set of data.

3. Redeploy the applications onto the simulators again. Once this is done, you
should see the watch face as shown in Figure 6.19.

Figure 6.19   The complications display the
upcoming movie name and its rating

Observe the name of the movie and the rating of 8.

Time Travel

One of the cool new features in watchOS 2 is Time Travel. Time Travel allows your application to display time-sensitive information on watch faces with complications. Let's modify our application so that it can display the titles of movies that were shown previously, as well as of movies that are coming up soon:

1. The getSupportedTimeTravelDirectionsForComplication:withHandler: method is already implemented by default:

```
func getSupportedTimeTravelDirectionsForComplication(
    complication: CLKComplication,
    withHandler handler: (CLKComplicationTimeTravelDirections) -> Void)
{
    handler([.Forward, .Backward])
}
```

This means your application will display complication data for past events as well as future events.

2. Next, add the following statement in bold to the getTimelineStartDate-ForComplication:withHandler: method:

```
func getTimelineStartDateForComplication(
    complication: CLKComplication,
    withHandler handler: (NSDate?) -> Void) {

    // handler(nil)
    //---the earliest date your complication can display data is 6 hours
    // ago---
    handler(NSDate(timeIntervalSinceNow: -6 * HOUR))
}
```

This means that you want to display complication data for events that happened up to six hours ago.

3. Add the following statements in bold to the getTimelineEndDateFor-Complication:withHandler: method:

```
func getTimelineEndDateForComplication(
    complication: CLKComplication,
    withHandler handler: (NSDate?) -> Void) {

    // handler(nil)
    //---the latest date your complication can display data is 12 hours
    // from now---
    handler(NSDate(timeIntervalSinceNow: 12 * HOUR))
}
```

This means that you want to display complication data for events that will happen up to 12 hours from now.

4. Add the following statements in bold to the getTimelineEntriesFor-Complication:beforeDate:limit:withHandler: method. This method is fired to obtain an array of CLKComplicationTimelineEntry objects, which will contain all the movies screened before the specified date (passed as an argument through the method).

```swift
func getTimelineEntriesForComplication(complication: CLKComplication,
        beforeDate date: NSDate, limit: Int,
        withHandler handler: (([CLKComplicationTimelineEntry]?) -> Void)) {
    // Call the handler with the timeline entries prior to the given
    // date.

    // handler(nil)
    var timelineEntries: [CLKComplicationTimelineEntry] = []

    //---find all movies before the current date---
    for movie in movies {
        if timelineEntries.count < limit &&
        movie.runningDate.timeIntervalSinceDate(date) < 0 {
            switch complication.family {
            case .ModularSmall:
                let modularSmallTemplate =
                CLKComplicationTemplateModularSmallRingText()

                modularSmallTemplate.textProvider =
                    CLKSimpleTextProvider(text: "\(Int(movie.rating))")

                modularSmallTemplate.fillFraction = movie.rating / 10

                modularSmallTemplate.ringStyle =
                    CLKComplicationRingStyle.Closed

                let entry = CLKComplicationTimelineEntry(
                    date:NSDate(timeInterval: 0 * MINUTE,
                        sinceDate: movie.runningDate),
                    complicationTemplate: modularSmallTemplate)
                timelineEntries.append(entry)

            case .ModularLarge:
                let modularLargeTemplate =
                    CLKComplicationTemplateModularLargeStandardBody()
                modularLargeTemplate.headerTextProvider =
                    CLKTimeIntervalTextProvider(
                        startDate: movie.runningDate,
                        endDate: NSDate(
                            timeInterval: movie.runningTime,
                            sinceDate: movie.runningDate))
```

```
                modularLargeTemplate.body1TextProvider =
                    CLKSimpleTextProvider(
                        text: movie.movieName,
                        shortText: movie.movieName)


                modularLargeTemplate.body2TextProvider =
                    CLKSimpleTextProvider(
                        text: "\(movie.runningTime / MINUTE) mins",
                        shortText: nil)


                let entry = CLKComplicationTimelineEntry(
                    date:NSDate(
                        timeInterval: 0 * MINUTE,
                        sinceDate: movie.runningDate),
                    complicationTemplate: modularLargeTemplate)


                timelineEntries.append(entry)

            case .UtilitarianSmall:
                break
            case .UtilitarianLarge:
                break
            case .CircularSmall:
                break
            }
        }
    }
    handler(timelineEntries)
}
```

The limit argument of the method indicates the maximum number of entries to provide. For efficiency, do not exceed the number of entries as specified.

5. Likewise, add the following statements in bold to the getTimelineEntries-ForComplication:afterDate:limit:withHandler: method. This method is fired to obtain an array of CLKComplicationTimelineEntry objects, which will contain all the movies screened after the specified date (passed as an argument through the method).

```
func getTimelineEntriesForComplication(complication: CLKComplication,
    afterDate date: NSDate, limit: Int,
    withHandler handler: (([CLKComplicationTimelineEntry]?) -> Void)) {
    // Call the handler with the timeline entries after the given
    // date.

    // handler(nil)
    var timelineEntries: [CLKComplicationTimelineEntry] = []

    //---find all movies after the current date---
    for movie in movies {
```

```
if timelineEntries.count < limit &&
movie.runningDate.timeIntervalSinceDate(date) > 0 {
    switch complication.family {
    case .ModularSmall:
        let modularSmallTemplate =
            CLKComplicationTemplateModularSmallRingText()

        modularSmallTemplate.textProvider =
            CLKSimpleTextProvider(text: "\(Int(movie.rating))")

        modularSmallTemplate.fillFraction = movie.rating / 10

        modularSmallTemplate.ringStyle =
            CLKComplicationRingStyle.Closed

        let entry = CLKComplicationTimelineEntry(
            date:NSDate(timeInterval: 0 * MINUTE,
            sinceDate: movie.runningDate),
            complicationTemplate: modularSmallTemplate)

        timelineEntries.append(entry)

    case .ModularLarge:
        let modularLargeTemplate =
            CLKComplicationTemplateModularLargeStandardBody()

        modularLargeTemplate.headerTextProvider =
            CLKTimeIntervalTextProvider(
                startDate: movie.runningDate,
                endDate: NSDate(timeInterval: movie.runningTime,
                    sinceDate: movie.runningDate))

        modularLargeTemplate.body1TextProvider =
            CLKSimpleTextProvider(text: movie.movieName,
                shortText: movie.movieName)

        modularLargeTemplate.body2TextProvider =
            CLKSimpleTextProvider(
                text: "\(movie.runningTime / MINUTE) mins",
                shortText: nil)

        let entry =
        CLKComplicationTimelineEntry(
            date:NSDate(
                timeInterval: 0 * MINUTE,
                sinceDate: movie.runningDate),
            complicationTemplate: modularLargeTemplate)

        timelineEntries.append(entry)
```

```
            case .UtilitarianSmall:
                break
            case .UtilitarianLarge:
                break
            case .CircularSmall:
                break
            }
        }
    }
    handler(timelineEntries)
}
```

6. That's it! Deploy the applications onto the simulators again.

7. This time, turn the scroll wheel on your mouse to activate Time Travel. Turning back a few minutes displays *World War Z*, and turning back more than two hours displays *Terminator 2* (see Figure 6.20, top).

8. Move the time forward about two hours and you should see *The Dark Knight*, and moving forward about six hours displays *The Prestige* (see Figure 6.20, bottom).

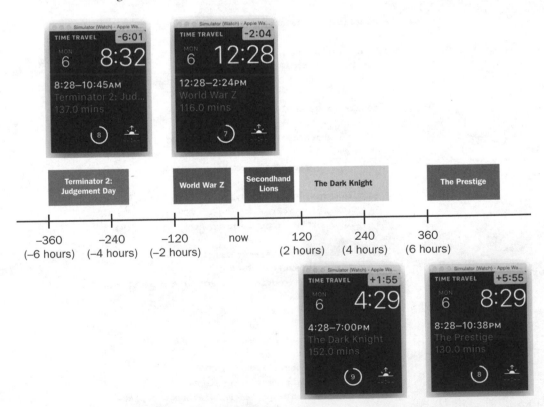

Figure 6.20   Timeline for the various movies past and future

Setting the Refresh Frequency

So, how often does the complication data get refreshed? You can programmatically specify how often ClockKit wakes up your application to request some data by implementing the getNextRequestedUpdateDateWithHandler: method:

```
func getNextRequestedUpdateDateWithHandler(handler: (NSDate?) -> Void) {
    // Call the handler with the date when you would next like to be
    // given the opportunity to update your complication content.

    // handler(nil);
    //---update in the next 1 hour---
    handler(NSDate(timeIntervalSinceNow: HOUR))
}
```

In the previous statement, you indicated that the complication data should be requested every hour. However, this is entirely up to ClockKit, and hence it is not guaranteed. Apple, however, does recommend that you refresh your complication data either hourly or daily, and that each time you refresh you should fetch as much information as you need for each fetch cycle.

If your WatchKit Extension app notices that the complication data is stale, you can also force a manual refresh using the CLKComplicationServer class, like this:

```
import ClockKit
...

    let complicationServer = CLKComplicationServer.sharedInstance()
    for complication in complicationServer.activeComplications {
        complicationServer.reloadTimelineForComplication(complication)
    }
```

> **Note**
>
> Although you can programmatically force a refresh of your complication data, iOS internally allocates a limit as to how often your app can refresh its data. Once the limit is reached, your app will not be able to refresh until the next day. This feature is to enhance the battery life of the Apple Watch.

Summary

In this chapter, you saw what complications are and how they can be implemented in your application. You learned how to display some real data and implement Time Travel, which is a feature in watchOS 2 that allows users to use the Digital Crown to scroll through time-sensitive complication data on the various watch faces.

7

Interfacing with iOS Apps

For the past 33 years, I have looked in the mirror every morning and asked myself: "If today were the last day of my life, would I want to do what I am about to do today?" And whenever the answer has been "No" for too many days in a row, I know I need to change something.

Steve Jobs

In watchOS 2, Apple has changed the execution model of the Apple Watch app. Instead of the logic of the watch app being executed on the iPhone, in watchOS 2 the logic is run on the watch itself. While this change is much welcomed (as the performance of apps is drastically improved), it presents another challenge to the developer: How do you communicate between the containing iOS app and the watch app? In watchOS 1, you communicate using the shared app group feature; however, this feature is no longer relevant in the new execution model of watchOS 2. Fortunately, WatchKit for watchOS 2 comes with a new framework: the *Watch Connectivity Framework*, which contains a set of APIs that allow the containing iOS app to communicate with the watch app (and vice versa). That is the subject of this chapter.

In addition to discussing how apps intercommunicate, this chapter also talks about how to use location services in your watch app, as well as how to consume web services. Last, but not least, this chapter ends with a discussion on persisting data on your watch app.

Introducing the Watch Connectivity Framework

In Chapter 1, "Getting Started with WatchKit Programming," you learned that to communicate between the containing iOS app and the Apple Watch app, you make use of the Watch Connectivity Framework. The Watch Connectivity Framework provides a two-way communication channel between the iOS app and the watch app. Using this framework, you can perform two key types of communication:

- **Background transfers**: Data/files are sent to the recipient in the background and are available when the recipient app launches.
- **Live communication**: Data is sent directly to the recipient app, which is currently active or launched to receive the data.

> **Note**
>
> Recipient here refers to either the iOS app or the Apple Watch app.

The next section elaborates on these two types of communication.

Types of Communication

For background transfers, the Watch Connectivity Framework supports three communication modes:

- Application Context
- User Info
- File Transfer

For the *Application Context* mode, you can send the most recent state information to the recipient. Figure 7.1 shows an example where the iOS app sends a series of dictionaries

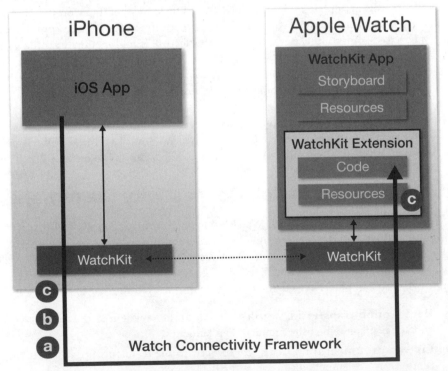

Figure 7.1 Sending data using the Application Context mode

(a, b, and c) to the Apple Watch. However, only the most recently sent dictionary is delivered to the watch app when it launches. This mode is useful for updating the state of your application, such as updating glances to display the most recent information about your app.

Note

Chapter 9, "Displaying Glances," contains an example of using the Application Context mode to send glance information.

Note

Note that the Watch Connectivity Framework is bidirectional—you can send data from the iPhone app to the Apple Watch app, and vice versa.

For the *User Info* mode, all data (dictionaries) is delivered in the same order in which it was sent (see Figure 7.2). This mode is useful if you need to continually send a series

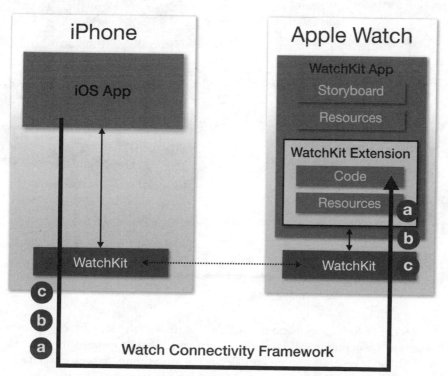

Figure 7.2 Sending data using the User Info mode

of data to the recipient (for example, sending a series of location coordinates to the iPhone for logging purposes).

For the *File Transfer* mode, you can transfer a file together with an optional dictionary to the recipient (see Figure 7.3). The file is transferred asynchronously in the background and saved in the ~/Documents/Inbox directory of the recipient. Once the recipient has been notified of an incoming file, the file is deleted automatically. This mode is useful for cases where you need to transfer files such as images to the recipient.

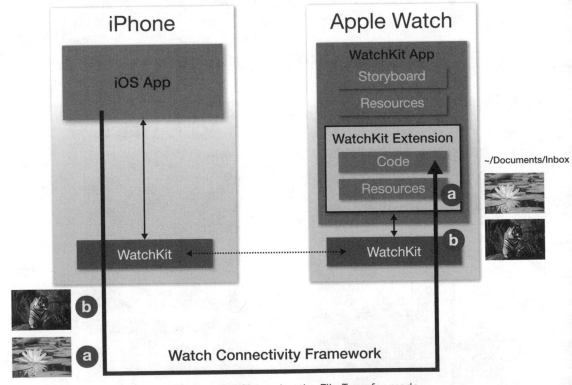

Figure 7.3 Sending files using the File Transfer mode

Besides the various background transfer modes, the Watch Connectivity Framework also supports live communication. For live communication, it supports the *Send Message* mode. This mode requires apps on both devices to be running. You can send data to the recipient and optionally request a reply from the recipient (see Figure 7.4).

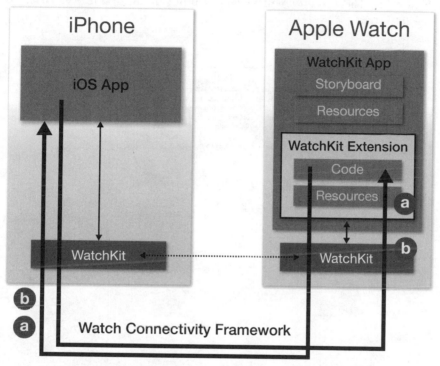

Figure 7.4 Sending live data using the Send Message mode

In the event the recipient is not running when you send data using the Send Message mode, the following happens:

- If you are sending data from the watch app, it triggers the corresponding iPhone app and launches it in the background to receive the data.

- If you are sending data from the iPhone app, it returns with an error indicating that the recipient is not reachable. You need to launch the watch app in order to receive the data.

Using the Watch Connectivity Framework

Now that you have a better understanding of how the Watch Connectivity Framework works, it is time to put it into action:

1. Using Xcode, create a new iOS App with WatchKit App project and name it **Communications**. Uncheck the option Include Notification Scene so that we can keep the WatchKit project to a bare minimum.

2. In the Main.storyboard file in the iOS project, add a TextView to the View window (for simplicity I have set this to the size of a 4.7-inch iPhone) and then set its Background attribute to **Group Table View Background Color** (see Figure 7.5). The TextView will be used to display all the data received from the Apple Watch.

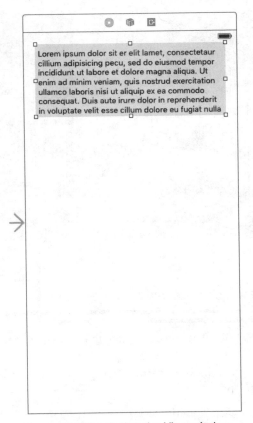

Figure 7.5 Populating the View window

3. Create an outlet for the TextView in ViewController.swift and connect it to the TextView:

```
import UIKit

class ViewController: UIViewController {

    @IBOutlet weak var textView: UITextView!
```

Sending Data Using Application Context

The first example shows how to send data from the Apple Watch to the containing iOS app using the Application Context mode.

In the WatchKit Extension

In the following steps, you modify the WatchKit Extension to send data from the Apple Watch app to the iOS app.

1. Add the following statements in bold to the InterfaceController.swift file:

```
import WatchKit
import Foundation
import WatchConnectivity

class InterfaceController: WKInterfaceController, WCSessionDelegate {

    override func awakeWithContext(context: AnyObject?) {
        super.awakeWithContext(context)

        // Configure interface objects here.

        if (WCSession.isSupported()) {
            let session = WCSession.defaultSession()
            session.delegate = self
            session.activateSession()

            //---on the watch, reachable is true if the iPhone is reachable
            // via Bluetooth---
            print("iPhone reachable: \(session.reachable)")
        }
    }
```

By adding these statements, you

- Imported the WatchConnectivity framework to the project.
- Made the InterfaceController class implement the WCSessionDelegate protocol. This protocol contains various methods that are fired when the watch receives incoming data from the iPhone.
- Created a session using the defaultSession method from the WCSession class. You then set its delegate property so that it knows the ViewController class will handle the methods fired by the WCSession class. When you are ready to receive incoming data, you call the activateSession method.
- Used the reachable property to check if the iPhone is reachable. On the Apple Watch, this property returns true if the iPhone is reachable via Bluetooth.

> **Note**
>
> Whenever there is a change in reachability between the iPhone and the Apple Watch, the `WCSession` object fires the `sessionReachabilityDidChange:` method. You can implement this method to be notified of such a change.

2. In the Interface.storyboard file, add a Button control to the Interface Controller and then set its title to **Application Context** (see Figure 7.6).

Figure 7.6 Populating the Interface Controller

3. Create an action for the button in the InterfaceController.swift file:

```
import WatchKit
import Foundation
import WatchConnectivity

class InterfaceController: WKInterfaceController, WCSessionDelegate {

    @IBAction func btnAppContext() {
    }
```

4. Add the following statements in bold to the InterfaceController.swift file:

```
import WatchKit
import Foundation
import WatchConnectivity

class InterfaceController: WKInterfaceController, WCSessionDelegate {

    @IBAction func btnAppContext() {
        do {
            let applicationContext =
                ["key1":"watch",
                 "key2":"appcontext",
                 "time": "\(NSDate())"]
            try
                WCSession.defaultSession().updateApplicationContext(
                    applicationContext)
```

```
    } catch {
        print("\(error)")
    }
}
```

In these statements, you

- Created a dictionary containing three keys: key1, key2, and time
- Used the updateApplicationContext: method of the WKSession object to send the dictionary to the iPhone

In the iOS App

In the following, you modify the iOS app to receive data from the Apple Watch app. Add the following statements in bold to the ViewController.swift file:

```
import UIKit

import WatchConnectivity

class ViewController: UIViewController, WCSessionDelegate {

    @IBOutlet weak var textView: UITextView!

    func updateTextView(message:String) {
        dispatch_async(dispatch_get_main_queue()) {
            self.textView.text =  message + "\n" + self.textView.text
        }
    }

    override func viewDidLoad() {
        super.viewDidLoad()
        // Do any additional setup after loading the view, typically from a
        // nib.

        //---clear the TextView---
        textView.text = ""

        if (WCSession.isSupported()) {
            let session = WCSession.defaultSession()
            session.delegate = self
            session.activateSession()

            //---on the iPhone, reachable is true only if the watch is
            // reachable via Bluetooth and the watch app is in the
            // foreground---
            updateTextView("Apple Watch app reachable: " +
                "\(session.reachable)")
```

```
        updateTextView("Apple Watch paired: " +
            "\(session.paired)")
        updateTextView("Watch app installed: " +
            "\(session.watchAppInstalled)")
    }
}

func session(session: WCSession,
didReceiveApplicationContext applicationContext: [String : AnyObject]) {
    updateTextView(applicationContext["key1"]! as! String)
    updateTextView(applicationContext["key2"]! as! String)
    updateTextView(applicationContext["time"]! as! String)
}
```

By adding these statements, you

- Imported the `WatchConnectivity` framework to the project.
- Made the `ViewController` class implement the `WCSessionDelegate` protocol. This protocol contains various methods that are fired when the phone receives incoming data from the watch.
- Added a method named `updateTextView` to append data in the TextView. All data is added using the main thread. This is needed as all the methods in the `WCSessionDelegate` protocol are not called from the main thread. Hence, you need to use the `dispatch_async` method to update the TextView in the main thread.
- Used the `WCSession`'s `isSupported` method to check if the Watch Connectivity Framework is supported.
- Created a session using the `defaultSession` method from the `WCSession` class. You then set its `delegate` property so that it knows the `ViewController` class will handle the methods fired by the `WCSession` class. When you are ready to receive incoming data, you called the `activateSession` method.
- Used the `reachable` property to check if the Apple Watch is reachable. On the iPhone, this property returns `true` if the Apple Watch is reachable via Bluetooth and the watch app is running in the foreground.
- Used the `paired` property to check if the Apple Watch is paired.
- Used the `watchAppInstalled` property to check if the watch app is installed on the Apple Watch.
- Implemented the `session:didReceiveApplicationContext:` method. This method is called when the watch app sends context data to the iPhone. The context data is sent as a dictionary.

Testing the Applications

You are now ready to test the application:

1. Select the Communications WatchKit App scheme in Xcode and deploy the projects onto the iPhone and Apple Watch Simulators.

2. On the Apple Watch Simulator, click the **Application Context** button a couple of times. This proves that the iPhone will receive only the latest dictionary that was sent; all earlier dictionaries will be replaced by the last dictionary sent.

3. On the iPhone Simulator, launch the Communications application that has been installed on it. You should see something similar to Figure 7.7.

Figure 7.7 The iOS app receiving the data sent using the Application Context mode

Observe that on the iPhone, the iOS app prints out the values of the three keys: key1, key2, and time. All these keys are from the latest dictionary sent to the iPhone.

> **Note**
>
> In this mode, the previous dictionaries sent are always overridden by the latest one.

Sending Data Using User Info

The second example shows how you send data using the User Info mode.

In the WatchKit Extension

In the following steps, you modify the WatchKit Extension to send data from the Apple Watch app to the iOS app.

1. In the Interface Controller in the Interface.storyboard file, add a Button control (see Figure 7.8) and set its title to **User Info**.

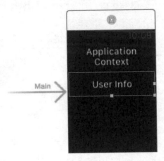

Figure 7.8 Populating the Interface Controller

2. Create an action for the button in the InterfaceController.swift file and connect it to the button:

```
import WatchKit
import Foundation
import WatchConnectivity

class InterfaceController: WKInterfaceController, WCSessionDelegate {

    @IBAction func btnUserInfo() {
    }
```

3. Add the following statements in bold to the InterfaceController.swift file:

```
import WatchKit
import Foundation
import WatchConnectivity

class InterfaceController: WKInterfaceController, WCSessionDelegate {

    @IBAction func btnUserInfo() {
        let userInfo = [
            "key1": "watch",
            "key2":"userinfo",
            "time": "\(NSDate())"
        ]
```

```
        let infoTransfer =
            WCSession.defaultSession().transferUserInfo(userInfo)
        print("Transferring: \(infoTransfer.transferring)")
    }

    func session(session: WCSession,
        didFinishUserInfoTransfer userInfoTransfer:
        WCSessionUserInfoTransfer,
        error: NSError?) {
        if error == nil {
            print("Transfer completed")
        } else {
            print("\(error)")
        }
    }
```

In the previous statements, you

- Created a dictionary containing three keys: key1, key2, and time.

- Used the transferUserInfo: method of the WKSession object to send the dictionary to the iPhone. This method returns a WCSessionUserInfoTransfer object, which you can use to check the status of the transfer (via the transferring property).

- Implemented the session:didFinishUserInfoTransfer:error: method. This method is fired when the transfer is completed, or if an error occurred during the transfer process.

In the iOS App

Here you modify the iOS app to receive data from the Apple Watch app. Add the following statements in bold to the ViewController.swift file:

```
import UIKit

import WatchConnectivity

class ViewController: UIViewController, WCSessionDelegate {

    @IBOutlet weak var textView: UITextView!

    func session(session: WCSession,
    didReceiveApplicationContext applicationContext: [String : AnyObject]) {
        ...
    }

    func session(session: WCSession,
    didReceiveUserInfo userInfo: [String : AnyObject]) {
        updateTextView(userInfo["key1"]! as! String)
```

```
        updateTextView(userInfo["key2"]! as! String)
        updateTextView(userInfo["time"]! as! String)
    }
```

The `session:didReceiveUserInfo:` method is fired when the user info data is received from the watch. The incoming data is passed as a dictionary.

Testing the Applications

You are now ready to test the application:

1. Select the Communications WatchKit App scheme in Xcode and deploy the projects onto the iPhone and Apple Watch Simulators.

2. On the Apple Watch Simulator, click the **User Info** button a couple of times. This proves that all data sent via this method is queued for delivery to the iPhone.

3. On the iPhone Simulator, launch the Communications application that has been installed on it. You should see something similar to Figure 7.9. Observe that you will receive multiple sets of the data (one for each click on the **User Info** button).

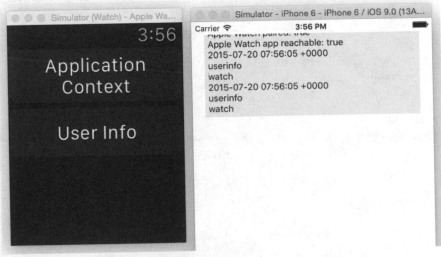

Figure 7.9 Receiving the data sent using the User Info mode

> **Note**
> Dictionaries sent using this method are delivered in the order in which they are sent.

Sending Data/Files Using File Transfer

In the third example, you transfer files.

In the WatchKit Extension

In the following steps, you modify the WatchKit Extension to send data from the Apple Watch app to the iOS app:

1. Drag and drop an image named emoji.png onto the **Communications WatchKit Extension** target (see Figure 7.10).

Figure 7.10 Adding an image to the Extension

2. In the Interface Controller in the Interface.storyboard file, add a Button control (see Figure 7.11) and set its title to **File Transfer**.

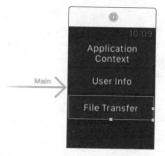

Figure 7.11 Populating the Interface Controller

3. Create an action for the button in the InterfaceController.swift file:

```
import WatchKit
import Foundation
import WatchConnectivity

class InterfaceController: WKInterfaceController, WCSessionDelegate {

    @IBAction func btnFileTransfer() {
    }
```

4. Add the following statements in bold to the InterfaceController.swift file:

```
import WatchKit
import Foundation
import WatchConnectivity

class InterfaceController: WKInterfaceController, WCSessionDelegate {

    @IBAction func btnFileTransfer() {
        let filePathURL:NSURL =
            NSURL(fileURLWithPath:
                NSBundle.mainBundle().pathForResource(
                    "emoji",
                    ofType: "png")!)

        let data = [
            "key1": "watch",
            "key2":"filetransfer",
            "time": "\(NSDate())"
        ]
        let fileTransfer = WCSession.defaultSession().transferFile(
            filePathURL, metadata:data)
        print("Transferring: \(fileTransfer.transferring)")
    }

    func session(session: WCSession,
    didFinishFileTransfer fileTransfer: WCSessionFileTransfer,
    error: NSError?) {
        if error == nil {
            print("Transfer completed")
        } else {
            print("\(error)")
        }
    }
}
```

In the previous statements, you

- Created a path to point to the emoji.png file located in the Extension bundle.
- Created a dictionary containing three keys: key1, key2, and time.

- Used the `transferFile:` method of the `WKSession` object to send the image and dictionary to the iPhone. This method returns a `WCSessionFileTransfer` object, which you can use to check the status of the transfer (via the `transferring` property).

- Implemented the `session:didFinishFileTransfer:error:` method. This method is fired when the transfer is completed, or if an error occurred during the transfer process.

In the iOS App

In the following steps, you modify the iOS app to receive data from the Apple Watch app:

1. In the Main.storyboard file, add an ImageView (see Figure 7.12) to the View window and set its Mode attribute to **Aspect Fit**.

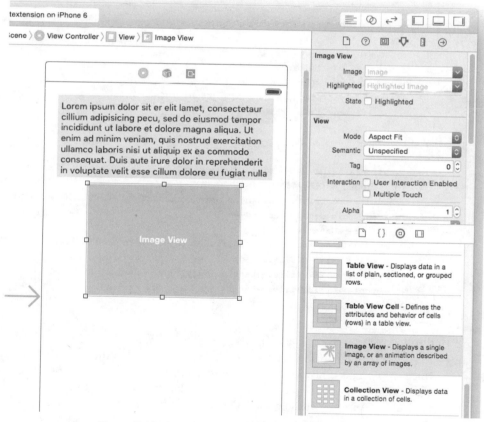

Figure 7.12 Adding the ImageView to the View window

2. Create an outlet for the ImageView in the ViewController.swift file and connect it to the ImageView:

```swift
import UIKit

import WatchConnectivity

class ViewController: UIViewController, WCSessionDelegate {

    @IBOutlet weak var textView: UITextView!
    @IBOutlet weak var image: UIImageView!
```

3. Add the following statements in bold to the ViewController.swift file:

```swift
import UIKit

import WatchConnectivity

class ViewController: UIViewController, WCSessionDelegate {

    @IBOutlet weak var textView: UITextView!
    @IBOutlet weak var image: UIImageView!
    func updateImageView(image:UIImage!) {
        dispatch_async(dispatch_get_main_queue()) {
            self.image.image = image
        }
    }

    func session(session: WCSession, didReceiveFile file: WCSessionFile) {
        let fileURL = file.fileURL
        //---move the file to somewhere more permanent as it will be deleted
        // after this method returns---
        if file.metadata != nil {
            updateImageView(UIImage(data: NSData(contentsOfURL: fileURL)!))
            updateTextView(file.metadata!["key1"] as! String)
            updateTextView(file.metadata!["key2"] as! String)
            updateTextView(file.metadata!["time"] as! String)
        }
    }
}
```

In this step, you

- Added a method named `updateImageView:` to display an image in the ImageView. This is necessary, as all the methods in the `WCSessionDelegate` protocol are not called from the main thread. Hence, you need to use the `dispatch_async` method to update the ImageView in the main thread.

- Implemented the `session:didReceiveFile:` method. This method is called when the watch app sends a file (with an optional dictionary) to the iPhone. The file is made available through the `WCSessionFile` object. You can load it via its `fileURL` property.

> **Note**
>
> The file that is transferred into the current device will be deleted after the `session:didReceiveFile:` method exits. Hence, you need to move it to somewhere more permanent (such as the Documents folder) if you need to use it later on.

Testing the Application

You are now ready to test the application:

1. Select the Communications WatchKit App scheme in Xcode and deploy the projects onto the iPhone and Apple Watch Simulators.

2. On the Apple Watch Simulator, click the **File Transfer** button a couple of times. This proves that all data sent via this method is queued for delivery to the iPhone.

3. On the iPhone Simulator, launch the Communications application that has been installed on it. You should see something similar to Figure 7.13. Observe that you will receive multiple sets of the data (one for each click on the **File Transfer** button).

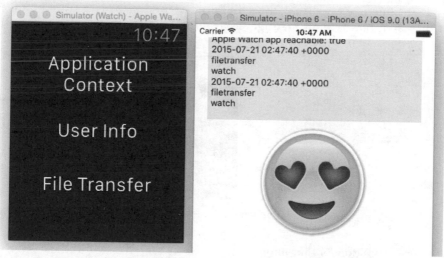

Figure 7.13 Receiving the file and the data sent using the File Transfer mode

Canceling Outstanding Transfers

The `WKSession` object allows you to obtain a list of outstanding File Transfer and User Info transfers:

```
let outstandingFileTransfers =
    WCSession.defaultSession().outstandingFileTransfers
let outstandingUserInfoTransfers =
    WCSession.defaultSession().outstandingUserInfoTransfers
```

The `outstandingFileTransfers` and `outstandingUserInfoTransfers` methods return an array of `WKSessionFileTransfer` and `WKSessionUserInfoTransfer` objects, respectively. Using this array of objects, you can cancel the transfer using the `cancel` method:

```
for transfer in outstandingFileTransfers {
    transfer.cancel()
}
for transfer in outstandingUserInfoTransfers {
    transfer.cancel()
}
```

Using Interactive Messaging

In this final example, you implement the Interactive Messaging mode.

In the WatchKit Extension

In the following steps, you modify the WatchKit Extension to send data from the Apple Watch app to the iOS app:

1. In the Interface.storyboard file, add a Button control to the Interface Controller and set its title to **Send Message** (see Figure 7.14).

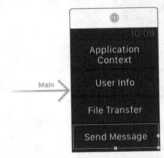

Figure 7.14 Populating the Interface Controller

2. Create an action for the button in the InterfaceController.swift file and connect it to the button:

```
import WatchKit
import Foundation
import WatchConnectivity

class InterfaceController: WKInterfaceController, WCSessionDelegate {

    @IBAction func btnSendMessage() {
    }
```

3. Add the following statements in bold to the InterfaceController.swift file:

```
import WatchKit
import Foundation

import WatchConnectivity

class InterfaceController: WKInterfaceController, WCSessionDelegate {

    @IBAction func btnSendMessage() {
        let message = [
            "key1":"watch",
            "key2":"sendmessage",
            "time": "\(NSDate())"
        ]

        //---send a message to the iPhone and wait for a reply---
        WCSession.defaultSession().sendMessage(message,
            replyHandler: { (replies) -> Void in
                print(replies["key1"])
                print(replies["key2"])
                print(replies["time"])
        }) { (error) -> Void in
            print("\(error)")
        }
    }
}
```

In these statements, you

- Created a dictionary containing three keys: key1, key2, and time.
- Used the sendMessage: method to send a dictionary to the iPhone. You specified a replyHandler closure, which will be executed asynchronously in a background thread. This closure is called when the recipient returns the data back to the current device. If you don't need a reply from the recipient, you can simply set the replyHandler to nil, like this:

```
//---send a message to the iPhone---
WCSession.defaultSession().sendMessage(message,
replyHandler: nil)
    { (error) -> Void in
        print("\(error)")
}
```

In the iOS App

In the following, you modify the iOS app to receive data from the Apple Watch app. Add the following statements in bold to the ViewController.swift file:

```
import UIKit

import WatchConnectivity
```

```
class ViewController: UIViewController, WCSessionDelegate {

    @IBOutlet weak var textView: UITextView!
    @IBOutlet weak var image: UIImageView!

    //---when a message arrives from the watch and needs a response---
    func session(session: WCSession,
    didReceiveMessage message: [String : AnyObject],
    replyHandler: ([String : AnyObject]) -> Void) {
        updateTextView("session:didReceiveMessage:replyHandler:")
        updateTextView(message["key1"]! as! String)
        updateTextView(message["key2"]! as! String)
        updateTextView(message["time"]! as! String)

        let reply = [
            "key1":"phone",
            "key2":"replymessage",
            "time": "\(NSDate())"
        ]
        replyHandler(reply)
    }

    //---when a message arrives from the watch and no response is needed---
    func session(session: WCSession,
    didReceiveMessage message: [String : AnyObject]) {
        updateTextView("session:didReceiveMessage:")
        updateTextView(message["key1"]! as! String)
        updateTextView(message["key2"]! as! String)
        updateTextView(message["time"]! as! String)
    }
```

In these statements, you

- Implemented the session:didReceiveMessage:replyHandler: method. This method is called when the watch app sends a message to the iPhone with the replyHandler set to a closure. To reply to the sender, simply pass a dictionary to the replyHandler.

- Implemented the session:didReceiveMessage: method. This method is called when the watch app sends a message to the iPhone with the replyHandler set to nil.

Testing the Application

You are now ready to test the application:

1. Select the Communications WatchKit App scheme in Xcode and deploy the projects onto the iPhone and Apple Watch Simulators.

2. On the Apple Watch Simulator, click the **Send Message** button. Observe the result printed in the Output window (see Figure 7.15). The iPhone application is

launched in the background, and after receiving the data from the watch, it sends back a reply.

Figure 7.15   Sending a message to the iOS app and getting a reply from it

Comparing the Different Modes

Now that you have seen the various communication modes in action, let's summarize their characteristics and differences. Table 7.1 summarizes the various key points of the four different modes of communication.

Table 7.1   **Comparing the Four Different Communication Modes**

| | Background Transfers | | | Interactive Messaging |
	Application Context	User Info	Send File	Send Message
What is sent?	Dictionaries are sent to the recipient and the latest dictionary always replaces the previous one.	Dictionaries are sent to the recipient and queued.	File paths and dictionaries are sent to the recipient and queued.	Dictionaries are sent to the recipient and queued.
Must recipient be running?	Recipient need not be running.	Recipient need not be running.	Recipient need not be running.	Sending a message from the Apple Watch to the iPhone wakes up the iPhone app In the background. Sending a message from the iPhone to the Apple Watch does not wake up the WatchKit Extension.
What is delivered?	Only the latest dictionary is delivered to the recipient when it runs.	All dictionaries are delivered in the order in which they were sent to the recipient when it runs.	Files are transferred to the recipient asynchronously in the background. Files and dictionaries are guaranteed to be delivered in the order in which they were sent to the recipient when it runs.	All dictionaries are delivered in the order in which they were sent to the recipient.
Getting a reply	One-way communication.	One-way communication.	One-way communication.	You can optionally specify a reply handler so that the recipient can return a dictionary back to you.
Use cases	Useful for updating application state, such as glances on the Apple Watch.	Useful for games where changes on one device must be synchronized on the other device.	Useful for transferring files between devices.	Useful for cases where you need to control your iPhone through the Apple Watch. For example, you can create an app on the Apple Watch to adjust the volume on the iPhone.

Connecting to the Outside World

One of the key features of making a mobile app is the ability to connect to the outside world and consume external data, and the Apple Watch app is no exception. In this section, you learn how to obtain location data on the Apple Watch as well as consume web services.

Getting Location Data

In watchOS 2, the CLLocationManager class has a new method called request-Location. Instead of getting a continuous stream of locations, the requestLocation method requests a single location update. The following example shows how you can use it to obtain the user's location.

> **Note**
>
> The CLLocationManager class in watchOS does not support the startUpdating-Location method, which is commonly used in the iOS platform.

1. Using Xcode, create a new iOS App with WatchKit App project and name it **UsingLocation**. Uncheck the option Include Notification Scene so that we can keep the WatchKit project to a bare minimum.

2. In the Info.plist file from the UsingLocation project (the iPhone app), add a new key and set its value as shown in Figure 7.16. The value of the NSLocation-WhenInUseUsageDescription key is displayed to the user when the iPhone app requests permission to use his or her location.

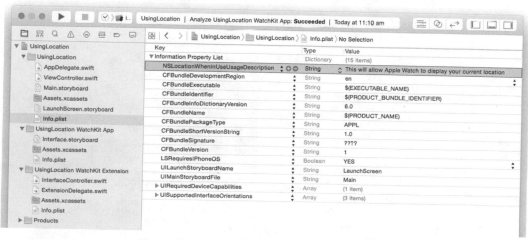

Figure 7.16   Adding a new key to the Info.plist file

3. Add the following statements in bold to the AppDelegate.swift file:

```
import UIKit
import CoreLocation

@UIApplicationMain
class AppDelegate: UIResponder, UIApplicationDelegate {

    var window: UIWindow?

    var lm: CLLocationManager!

    func application(application: UIApplication,
    didFinishLaunchingWithOptions launchOptions: [NSObject: AnyObject]?) ->
    Bool {
        // Override point for customization after application launch.

        lm = CLLocationManager()
        lm.requestWhenInUseAuthorization()

        return true
    }
```

The requestWhenInUseAuthorization method requests permission to use the location services whenever the application is in the foreground. This call is necessary in order for the Apple Watch to obtain the user's current location.

4. In the Interface.storyboard file, add the following controls onto the Interface Controller (see Figure 7.17):

- Label
- Button

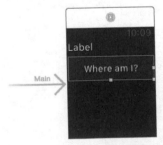

Figure 7.17   Populating the Interface Controller

5. In the InterfaceController.swift file, create the following outlets and actions and connect them to the controls in the Interface Controller:

```
import WatchKit
import Foundation

class InterfaceController: WKInterfaceController {

    @IBOutlet var label: WKInterfaceLabel!
    @IBAction func btnWhereAmI() {
    }
```

6. Add the following statements in bold to the InterfaceController.swift file:

```
import WatchKit
import Foundation
import CoreLocation

class InterfaceController: WKInterfaceController, CLLocationManagerDelegate {
    var lm: CLLocationManager!
    @IBOutlet var label: WKInterfaceLabel!

    @IBAction func btnWhereAmI() {
        lm.requestLocation()
    }

    override func awakeWithContext(context: AnyObject?) {
        super.awakeWithContext(context)

        // Configure interface objects here.
        lm = CLLocationManager()
        lm.delegate = self
        lm.desiredAccuracy = kCLLocationAccuracyBest
    }

    func locationManager(manager: CLLocationManager,
    didUpdateLocations locations: [CLLocation]) {
        //---get the most recent location---
        let currentLocation = locations.last!
        let str = "\(currentLocation.coordinate.latitude), " +
                  "\(currentLocation.coordinate.longitude)"
        print(str)
    }

    func locationManager(manager: CLLocationManager,
    didChangeAuthorizationStatus status: CLAuthorizationStatus) {
```

```
    switch status.rawValue {
        case 0: label.setText("[NotDetermined]")
        case 1: label.setText("[Restricted]")
        case 2: label.setText("[Denied]")
        case 3: label.setText("[AuthorizedAlways]")
        case 4: label.setText("[AuthorizedWhenInUse]")
        default:break
    }
}

func locationManager(manager: CLLocationManager,
didFailWithError error: NSError) {
    print("\(error)")
}
```

In the previous statements, you

- First created an instance of the CLLocationManager class and set the delegate to self so that you can implement methods fired by the CLLocationManager class.

- Implemented the locationManager:didUpdateLocations: method. This method is fired whenever the CLLocationManager class manages to find your latest location.

- Implemented the locationManager:didFailWithError: method. This method is fired whenever the CLLocationManager class is not able to find the current location.

- Implemented the locationManager:didChangeAuthorizationStatus: method. This method is fired whenever the status of the location authorization has changed.

- Used the requestLocation method to request the location manager to return the current location (single location). Once the location is obtained (in the locationManager:didUpdateLocations: method), you print out the location.

7. Select the UsingLocation WatchKit App scheme in Xcode and deploy the projects onto the iPhone and Apple Watch Simulators. On the Apple Watch Simulator, you see that the location authorization status is not determined yet (see Figure 7.18). This is because you have not given the authorization on the iPhone app.

8. On the iPhone Simulator, launch the UsingLocation application that has been installed on it. You will now be asked for the permission (see Figure 7.19). Click **Allow**.

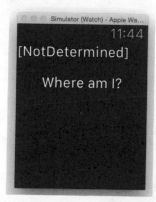

Figure 7.18   The location authorization
status is not determined yet

Figure 7.19   Giving permission on the iOS app

Once permission is granted to access the location, you see that the Apple Watch displays the authorization as **AuthorizedWhenInUse** (see Figure 7.20).

Figure 7.20   Once permission is granted on the iPhone, the authorization status changes on the watch app

9. With the iPhone Simulator selected, go to **Debug | Location** and select **Freeway Drive** (see Figure 7.21). This simulates the iPhone getting a series of locations.

10. On the Apple Watch Simulator, click the **Where am I?** button. You should see the latitude and longitude displayed in the Output window (see Figure 7.22).

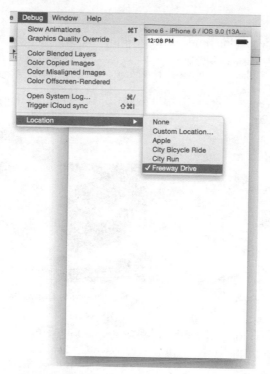

Figure 7.21   Simulating location changes
on the iPhone Simulator

Figure 7.22   Displaying the location
obtained in the Output window

Display Map

Knowing the latitude and longitude of your current location is not very helpful. A better way to represent the current location would be to display it on a map. This section shows you how to display a map using the Map control:

1. In the Interface.storyboard file, add the Map control onto the Interface Controller (see Figure 7.23).

Figure 7.23   Populating the Interface Controller

2. In the InterfaceController.swift file, create the following outlets and actions and connect them to the controls in the Interface Controller:

```
import WatchKit
import Foundation

class InterfaceController: WKInterfaceController {

    @IBOutlet var label: WKInterfaceLabel!
    @IBOutlet var map: WKInterfaceMap!
```

3. Add the following statements in bold to the InterfaceController.swift file:

```
override func awakeWithContext(context: AnyObject?) {
    super.awakeWithContext(context)

    // Configure interface objects here.
    lm = CLLocationManager()
    lm.delegate = self
    lm.desiredAccuracy = kCLLocationAccuracyBest
    map.setHidden(true)
}
func locationManager(manager: CLLocationManager,
didUpdateLocations locations: [CLLocation]) {
    //---get the most recent location---
    let currentLocation = locations.last! as CLLocation
```

```
    let str = "\(currentLocation.coordinate.latitude), " +
              "\(currentLocation.coordinate.longitude)"
    print(str)

    //---for displaying the map---
    let coordinateSpan =  MKCoordinateSpan(
        latitudeDelta: 0.010, longitudeDelta: 0.010)

    let loc = CLLocationCoordinate2D(
        latitude: currentLocation.coordinate.latitude,
        longitude: currentLocation.coordinate.longitude)

    map.setHidden(false)
    map.removeAllAnnotations()
    map.addAnnotation(loc, withPinColor: WKInterfaceMapPinColor.Purple)
    map.setRegion(MKCoordinateRegion(center: loc, span: coordinateSpan))
}
```

In these statements,

- You hid the map initially when the app was loaded.
- Once the location was obtained (in the `locationManager:didUpdate-Locations:` method), you displayed the location using the Map control.
- You added an annotation (a pushpin) to indicate the current location.

4. Select the UsingLocation WatchKit App scheme in Xcode and deploy the projects onto the iPhone and Apple Watch Simulators.

5. On the Apple Watch Simulator, click the **Where am I?** button. After a while, a map is shown with the location marked (see Figure 7.24).

Figure 7.24   Displaying the location using a Map

Note

The Map control displays a static map; you won't be able to pan the map. However, if you click on the Map control, you will be brought to another screen where you can get directions for walking or driving (see Figure 7.25, left). Scrolling to the bottom of the screen reveals the map (see Figure 7.25, center). Clicking on the map displays the built-in Maps app (see Figure 7.25, right), where you can pan the map.

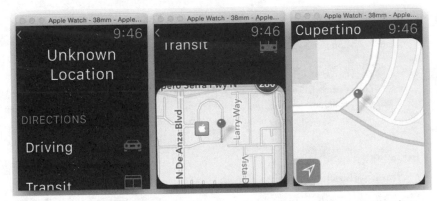

Figure 7.25   Clicking on the Map control launches the Maps application on the Apple Watch simulator, where you can pan the map

Accessing Web Services

In watchOS 2, because the Watch app runs directly on the Apple Watch, your app can now directly connect to the Internet without going through the iPhone. This is useful in situations where your watch is not within range of your iPhone, and this ability allows your application to remain connected with the outside world.

1. Using Xcode, create a new iOS App with WatchKit App project and name it **WebServices**. Uncheck the option Include Notification Scene so that we can keep the WatchKit project to a bare minimum.

2. Select the Interface.storyboard file to edit it in the Storyboard Editor.

3. Drag and drop a Button control (and set its title to **Get Weather**) onto the Interface Controller, as shown in Figure 7.26.

4. Create an action for the button in the InterfaceController.swift file:

```
import WatchKit
import Foundation

class InterfaceController: WKInterfaceController {

    @IBAction func btnGetWeather() {
    }
```

Figure 7.26   Populating the Interface Controller

5. Add the following statements in bold to the InterfaceController.swift file:

```swift
import WatchKit
import Foundation

class InterfaceController: WKInterfaceController {
    let INVALID_TEMP:Double = 9999
    //---parse the JSON string---
    func parseJSONData(data: NSData) -> Double {
            var parsedJSONData: NSDictionary!
        do {
            parsedJSONData = try NSJSONSerialization.JSONObjectWithData(data,
                options: NSJSONReadingOptions.MutableContainers) as!
                NSDictionary
        } catch {
            return INVALID_TEMP
        }

        let main = parsedJSONData["main"] as? NSDictionary
        if let temp = main {
            //---convert temperature to Celsius---
            return (temp["temp"] as! Double) - 273;
        } else {
            return INVALID_TEMP
        }
    }

    func displayAlert(title:String, message:String) {
        let okAction = WKAlertAction(title: "OK",
            style: WKAlertActionStyle.Default) { () -> Void in
                print("OK")
        }
        self.presentAlertControllerWithTitle(title,
            message: message,
            preferredStyle: WKAlertControllerStyle.Alert,
            actions: [okAction])
    }
```

```
@IBAction func btnGetWeather() {
    /*
    For http://, you need to add the following keys in Info.plist:
        NSAppTransportSecurity
            NSAllowsArbitraryLoads - YES
        Application Transport Security has blocked a cleartext HTTP
        (http://) resource load since it is insecure. Temporary exceptions
        can be configured via your app's Info.plist file.
    */
    let country = "Amsterdam"

    //---URL of the web service---
    let urlString = "http://api.openweathermap.org/data/2.5/weather?q=" +
        country

    let session = NSURLSession.sharedSession()

    session.dataTaskWithURL(NSURL(string:urlString)!,
        completionHandler: {
            (data, response, error) -> Void in
            let httpResp:NSHTTPURLResponse! = response as?
                NSHTTPURLResponse
            if httpResp != nil {
                if error == nil && httpResp.statusCode == 200 {
                    //---parse the JSON result---
                    let temp = self.parseJSONData(data!)
                    if temp < self.INVALID_TEMP {
                        self.displayAlert("Weather",
                            message:
                        "Weather in \(country) is \(temp) degrees Celsius")
                    } else {
                        self.displayAlert("Weather",
                            message: "No weather found")
                    }
                } else {
                    self.displayAlert("Error",
                        message: "\(error)")
                }
            } else {
                self.displayAlert("Error",
                    message: "Unable to contact web service")
            }
        }).resume()
}
```

In the previous statements, you

- Defined a function named parseJSONData: to take in an argument of type NSData (containing JSON content) and then extracted the temperature from it and returned the temperature as a double value

- Defined a function named displayAlert: to display an alert with the specified title and message

- Used the NSURLSession object to connect to a web service so that you can fetch the temperature of a city

6. In the Info.plist file in the Extension project, add the two keys NSAppTransport-Security and NSAllowsArbitraryLoads, as shown in Figure 7.27.

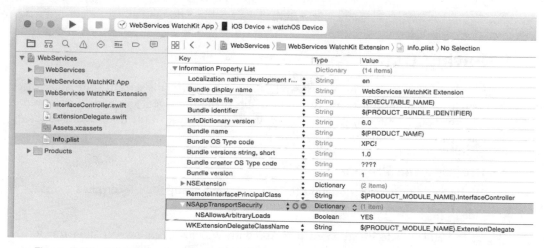

Figure 7.27   Adding the keys in Info.plist to allow access to web resources using http://

These two keys are needed so that your Watch app can connect to a web service using http:// instead of https:// (which is the default).

7. Select the WebServices WatchKit App scheme in Xcode and deploy the projects onto the iPhone and Apple Watch Simulators.

8. On the Apple Watch Simulator, click the **Get Weather** button. After a while, an alert appears, displaying the temperature of the specified city (see Figure 7.28).

> **Note**
>
> To prove that the Apple Watch app can continue to connect to the web service without the iPhone, deploy the application onto a real Apple Watch and iPhone. After that, turn on flight mode on the iPhone and run the application on the Apple Watch. You should still be able to get the weather of the specified city.

Figure 7.28   Getting the weather information

Saving Data

In this section, we briefly discuss two techniques for persisting data in your Apple Watch applications. First, you can write to a text file and save it into the Documents directory on your Apple Watch. Second, you can make use of the NSUserDefaults class to save key/value pairs.

Creating the Project

Let's create a project that prompts the user to enter a string (or select from a list of predefined strings):

1. Using Xcode, create a new iOS App with WatchKit App project and name it **FileStorage**. Uncheck the option Include Notification Scene so that we can keep the WatchKit project to a bare minimum.

2. Select the Interface.storyboard file to edit it in the Storyboard Editor.

3. Drag and drop the following controls onto the Interface Controller, as shown in Figure 7.29:

   - Three buttons
   - Label
   - Image

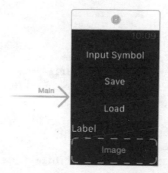

Figure 7.29   Populating the Interface Controller

4. Create the following outlets and actions in the InterfaceController.swift file:

```swift
import WatchKit
import Foundation

class InterfaceController: WKInterfaceController {

    @IBOutlet var image: WKInterfaceImage!
    @IBOutlet var label: WKInterfaceLabel!

    @IBAction func btnInputText() {
    }

    @IBAction func btnSave() {
    }

    @IBAction func btnLoad()   {
    }
```

Writing to Files

There are a few different methods you can use to save data to files. The first method is to write data to files. The `String` structure has a couple of methods that allow you to save the contents of the string into a file as well as load its contents from a file:

1. Add the following statements in bold to the InterfaceController.swift file:

```swift
import WatchKit
import Foundation

class InterfaceController: WKInterfaceController {

    var filePath:String!
    var symbol:String! = "[Symbol]"
```

```
@IBOutlet var image: WKInterfaceImage!
@IBOutlet var label: WKInterfaceLabel!

func displayAlert(title:String, message: String) {
    let okAction = WKAlertAction(title: "OK",
        style: WKAlertActionStyle.Default) { () -> Void in
            print("OK")
    }
    presentAlertControllerWithTitle(title,
        message: message,
        preferredStyle: WKAlertControllerStyle.Alert,
        actions: [okAction])
}

@IBAction func btnInputText() {
    presentTextInputControllerWithSuggestions(
        ["AAPL", "AMZN", "FB", "GOOG"],
        allowedInputMode: WKTextInputMode.AllowEmoji)
        { (results) -> Void in
            if results != nil {
                //---trying to see if the result can be converted
                // to String---
                self.symbol = results!.first as? String
                if self.symbol != nil {
                    self.label.setText(self.symbol!)
                }
            }
        }
}


@IBAction func btnSave() {
    do {
        try
            symbol.writeToFile(filePath,
                atomically: true,
                encoding: NSUTF8StringEncoding)
            displayAlert("Saved", message: "String saved successfully")
    } catch let error as NSError {
        displayAlert("Error", message: "\(error)")
    }
}

@IBAction func btnLoad()  {
    do {
        try
        symbol = String(contentsOfFile: filePath,
            encoding: NSUTF8StringEncoding)
```

```
        displayAlert("Retrieved", message: "Symbol is " + symbol)
    } catch let error as NSError {
        displayAlert("Error", message: "\(error)")
    }
}


override func awakeWithContext(context: AnyObject?) {
    super.awakeWithContext(context)

    // Configure interface objects here.
    if let dir : NSString = NSSearchPathForDirectoriesInDomains(
        NSSearchPathDirectory.DocumentDirectory,
        NSSearchPathDomainMask.AllDomainsMask, true).first {
        filePath = dir.stringByAppendingPathComponent("myfile.txt");
    }
}
```

In the `awakeWithContext:` method, you first created a path to a file named myfile.txt in the Documents directory. This file is used to save the contents of a string. You then used the `presentTextInputControllerWithSuggestions: allowedInputMode:` method to ask the user to input some text. When the text has been entered, it is displayed in the Label control. When the user clicks the **Save** button, you save the text using the `writeToFile:atomically:encoding:` method of the `String` structure. To load the text from the file, you use the initializer of the `String` structure.

2. Select the FileStorage WatchKit App scheme in Xcode and deploy the projects onto the iPhone and Apple Watch Simulators.

3. On the Apple Watch Simulator, click the **Input Symbol** button. Select a symbol (say, **AAPL**), and you should now see it displayed in the Label control (see Figure 7.30). Clicking the **Save** button saves the text into the watch. Clicking the **Load** button displays the contents of the saved file.

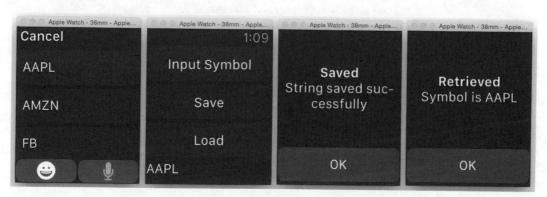

Figure 7.30   Saving the string using a file

Using `NSUserDefaults`

The file method is usually the easiest and best way to save string content. However, for storing structured data (such as key/value pairs), you are better off using the NSUserDefaults class:

1. Add the following statements in bold to the InterfaceController.swift file:

```
@IBAction func btnSave() {
    do {
        try
            symbol.writeToFile(filePath,
                atomically: true,
                encoding: NSUTF8StringEncoding)
            displayAlert("Saved", message: "String saved successfully")
    } catch let error as NSError {
        displayAlert("Error", message: "\(error)")
    }

    let defaults = NSUserDefaults.standardUserDefaults()
    defaults.setValue(symbol, forKey: "symbol")
    defaults.synchronize()
}


@IBAction func btnLoad()  {
    do {
        try
          symbol = String(contentsOfFile: filePath,
              encoding: NSUTF8StringEncoding)
          displayAlert("Retrieved", message: "Symbol is " + symbol)
    } catch let error as NSError {
        displayAlert("Error", message: "\(error)")
    }

    let defaults = NSUserDefaults.standardUserDefaults()
    let str = defaults.stringForKey("symbol")
    print("\(str)")
}
```

2. Select the FileStorage WatchKit App scheme in Xcode and deploy the projects onto the iPhone and Apple Watch Simulators.

3. On the Apple Watch Simulator, click the **Input Symbol** button. Select a symbol (say, **AAPL**), and you should now see it displayed in the Label control. Clicking the **Save** button saves the text onto the watch. Clicking the **Load** button displays the contents of the saved string in the Output window.

Summary

In this chapter, you saw how your Apple Watch app can communicate with the containing iOS through the various modes supported: Application Context, User Info, File Transfer, and Interactive Messaging. Each mode has its intended usage, which should be sufficient to satisfy most of your needs. In addition, you also learned how the watch app can communicate with the outside world even if the iPhone is not available. Finally, you saw two easy ways to persist data on your Apple Watch.

Displaying Notifications

*You can't connect the dots looking forward; you can only connect
them looking backwards. So you have to trust that the dots will
somehow connect in your future. You have to trust in something—
your gut, destiny, life, karma, whatever. This approach has never
let me down, and it has made all the difference in my life.*

Steve Jobs

By design, the Apple Watch is an extension of your iPhone. Instead of pulling the
iPhone out of your pocket, Apple wants you to look at and perform most of the tasks
on your Apple Watch. One of the most common ways a user interacts with the iPhone
is through notifications, and the Apple Watch supports that right out of the box.

When an iPhone is paired with an Apple Watch, notifications received by the
iPhone are sent to the Apple Watch. Your Apple Watch application then has the option
to display the notification to the user in more detail, and the user can also accomplish
actions associated with the notifications.

What Is a Notification?

A *notification* in iOS is a message that informs the user of some information that is coming in. For example, the Messages application may display a notification to inform you
that you have an incoming message from a friend, or you may receive a notification
informing you that you have a new email message on your mail server. Notifications
allow applications that are not running in the foreground to notify the user of new
data, and they allow app developers to write useful applications that work even if an
application is in the background.

On iOS, a user can receive two types of notifications:

- **Local notifications**: Notifications sent by the app itself. For example, an
  events-management application may schedule local notifications to be fired at
  different times to remind users of upcoming events.

- **Remote notifications** (also commonly known as *push notifications*): Notifications
  sent from outside the device. For example, a chat application sends a notification
  to a user when someone sends the user a message.

In iOS 8, Apple added interactive notifications so that you can directly act on a notification when you receive it. A good example is Gmail on the iPhone. The left panel of Figure 8.1 shows a notification about a new email message when the device is unlocked; the notification is shown as a banner at the top of the screen. If you touch the notification and drag it downward, you see two action buttons: **Reply** and **Archive** (see Figure 8.1, right).

Tapping the **Reply** button brings the Gmail application to the foreground so that you can reply to that email message. Tapping the **Archive** button directly archives the message without bringing Gmail to the foreground. An action button that brings the application to the foreground is known as a *foreground* action button. Likewise, an action button that does not bring the application to the foreground is known as a *background* action button. For both types of action buttons, you can configure whether the user must unlock the device before performing the action.

Figure 8.1   Receiving a notification from Gmail when the device is unlocked

Figure 8.2 shows the same notification received when the device is locked. Swiping the notification to the left reveals the two action buttons. The action button that performs destructive operations (such as deletion, archiving, etc.) is displayed in red.

When the notification is displayed as a banner, at most two action buttons are shown.

Figure 8.2   Receiving the notification when the device is locked

To display more than two action buttons, the notification must be configured to display as an alert. Figure 8.3 shows the same notification configured to display as an alert. Tapping the **Options** button (see Figure 8.3, left) displays another alert with the various action buttons (see Figure 8.3, right).

In Figure 8.3, you see the three action buttons (the first two of which you have already seen): **Open**, **Archive**, and **Reply**.

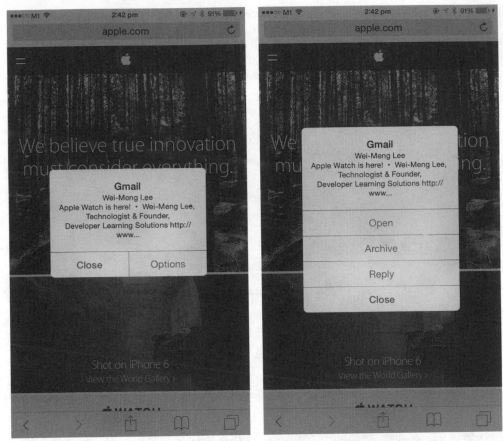

Figure 8.3   Displaying the notification as an alert

For this chapter, remember the following points about iOS notifications:

- Local notifications emanate from the application itself.
- Remote notifications come from outside the device.
- An action button can be either a foreground or background action button.
- An action button can be configured to perform an action only if the device is unlocked.
- An action button that performs destructive operations is displayed in red.

Types of Notifications on the Apple Watch

When notifications (local or remote) are received on the iPhone, iOS decides whether to display them on the iPhone or send them to the Apple Watch.

When the Apple Watch receives a notification, it notifies the user as follows:

- First, it displays the notification using a minimal interface, known as the *short-look interface*. The notification disappears when the user lowers his or her wrist.

- If the user's wrist remains raised or if the user taps the short-look interface, the *long-look interface* appears. The long-look interface displays the notification in more detail.

Note

If the iPhone is unlocked when a notification arrives, iOS assumes that the iPhone is being used and the notification shows on the iPhone. If the device is locked when the notification arrives, the notification goes to the Apple Watch instead.

For the short-look interface, you don't have to do much, as the interface is pretty restricted—you can just display the contents of the notification. For the long-look interface, you can customize the details of the notification by displaying additional text or images.

Implementing the Short-Look Interface

Let's look at how to implement the short-look interface for notifications:

1. Using Xcode, create a new iOS App with WatchKit App project and name it **Notifications**. Be sure to check the Include Notification Scene option (see Figure 8.4).

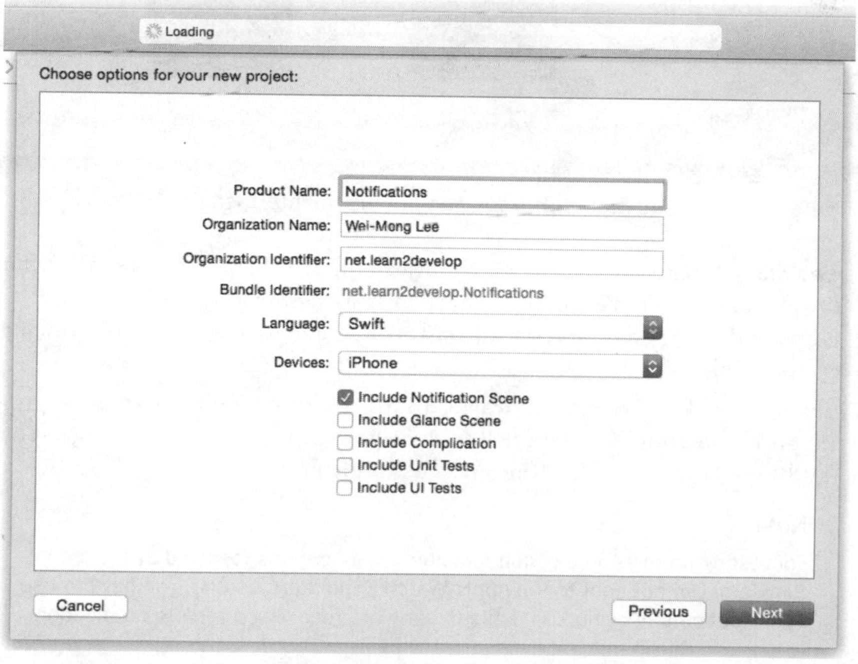

Figure 8.4   Creating a WatchKit app with the inclusion of the Notification Scene

2. Examine the Interface.storyboard file located in the WatchKit app (see Figure 8.5). Observe that, in addition to the Interface Controller, you now have two more controllers: Static Interface Controller and Dynamic Interface Controller.

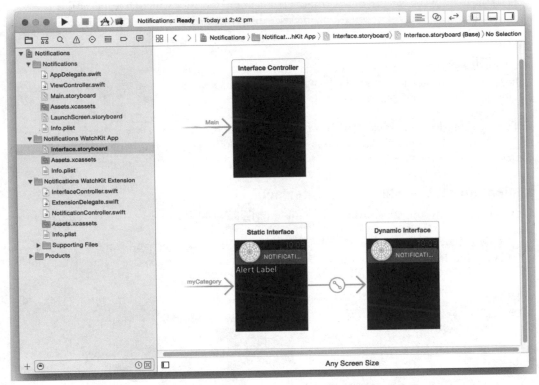

Figure 8.5   The storyboard with the two additional Interface Controllers

The Static Interface Controller is for displaying the short-look interface, whereas the Dynamic Interface Controller is for displaying the long-look interface. Observe that the Static Interface Controller contains a Label control, which is customizable.

3. Examine the PushNotificationPayload.apns file located in the Extension project's Support Files group (see Figure 8.6). It is used for simulating receiving a remote (push) notification on the Apple Watch Simulator.

> **Note**
>
> For testing on the Apple Watch Simulator, notifications received by the iPhone Simulator are not sent to the Apple Watch Simulator; instead, you have to use the PushNotificationPayload.apns file to simulate receiving a remote notification.

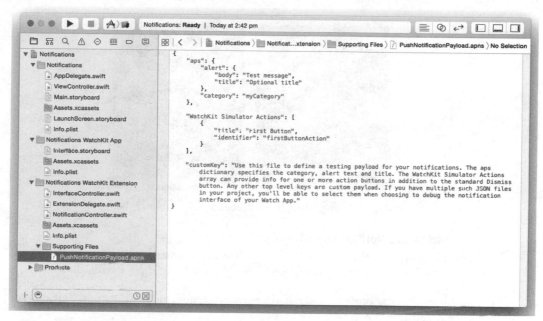

Figure 8.6 The PushNotificationPayload.apns file contains the payload of a remote notification

4. To test the application, select the **Notification – Notifications WatchKit App** scheme (see Figure 8.7) at the top of Xcode and run it on the iPhone Simulator.

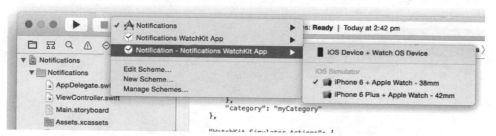

Figure 8.7   Selecting the notification scheme so that the payload can be used for the notification

You should see the Apple Watch Simulator displaying a screen containing the app icon, notification title, and app name, followed by the actual notification, as shown in Figure 8.8.

Observe that the Label control displays the text "Test Message," and the button displays the title "First Button"; both texts come from the PushNotificationPayload.apns file. The **Dismiss** button is always there, and clicking it dismisses the notification. Clicking **First Button** invokes the default Interface Controller on the WatchKit application.

Figure 8.8 Displaying the notification on the Apple Watch

Customizing the Notification Message

The Label control on the Static Interface Controller supports text containing line break characters (\n). You can use this to break a long line into multiple shorter lines:

1. Using the same project created in the previous section, modify the PushNotification-Payload.apns file as follows:

```
{
    "aps": {
        "alert": {
            "body":
            "Boarding Now\nFlight 164 to Los Angeles boards at 6:50AM at
              Gate 46",
            "title": "Boarding"
        },
        "category": "myCategory"
    },

    "WatchKit Simulator Actions": [
        {
            "title": "First Button",
            "identifier": "firstButtonAction"
        }
    ],

    "customKey": "Use this file to define a testing payload for your
    notifications. The aps dictionary specifies the category, alert text, and
    title. The WatchKit Simulator Actions array can provide info for one or
    more action buttons in addition to the standard Dismiss button. Any other
    top level keys are custom payload. If you have multiple such JSON files
    in your project, you'll be able to select them when choosing to debug the
    notification interface of your Watch App."
}
```

Note

The value of the `body` key in the PushNotificationPayload.apns file has been formatted for readability. When testing on the iPhone Simulator, it should be a continuous line: "Boarding Now\nFlight 164 to Los Angeles boards at 6:50AM at Gate 46."

2. In the Interface.storyboard file, set the Lines attribute of the Label control on the Static Interface Controller to **0** (see Figure 8.9).

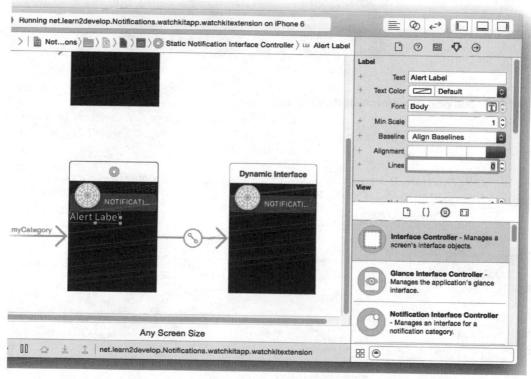

Figure 8.9   Setting the Lines attribute of the Label control to **0**

3. Run the application on the iPhone Simulator. On the opening screen, you should now see the "Boarding" word (see Figure 8.10, left). You should now also see the text on the Label control displayed in multiple lines (see Figure 8.10, right). To dismiss the notification, you can scroll the page upward and click the **Dismiss** button.

Note

You need to dismiss the previous notification (see Figure 8.8) before seeing the new notification.

Figure 8.10　The Label control displaying the text broken into multiple lines

Modifying the WatchKit Application Name

If you observe the right of Figure 8.10 carefully, you will notice that the Static Interface Controller is displaying the project name of "NOTIFICATION…" (part of it is truncated). You can change this to display a different name:

1. Select the Info.plist file located in the WatchKit app's Supporting Files group, and modify the value of the Bundle display name key to your desired app name, say, **Apple Air** (see Figure 8.11).

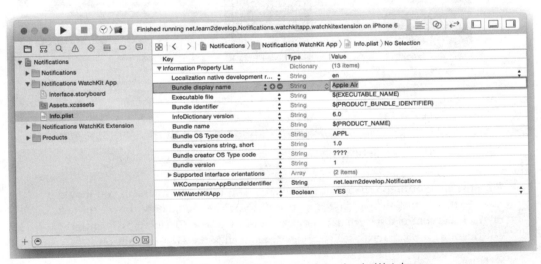

Figure 8.11　Changing the name of the Apple Watch app

2. Run the application on the iPhone Simulator, and you should now see both the opening screen and the Static Interface Controller with "Apple Air" in all capital letters (see Figure 8.12).

Figure 8.12   The name of the Apple Watch app is now changed

Setting Icons for the Apple Watch App

All Apple Watch apps submitted to the App Store must have icons. To create an icon, you need to prepare an image in various sizes and then copy it into your project. These icons are then used in various places on the watch: Notification Center, Apple Watch Companion Settings, Home screen, short-look interface, and long-look interface.

1. Prepare a set of icons with the following names and dimensions:

icon48×48.png: 48×48 pixels

icon55×55.png: 55×55 pixels

icon58×58.png: 58×58 pixels

icon87×87.png: 87×87 pixels

icon80×80.png: 80×80 pixels

icon88×88.png: 88×88 pixels

icon172×172.png: 172×172 pixels

icon196×196.png: 196×196 pixels

> **Note**
>
> You can find a copy of these images in the source code download for this book.

2. Select the **Assets.xcassets** item in the WatchKit App and drag and drop the icons prepared in the previous step onto each of the placeholders as shown in Figure 8.13 (follow the order listed in the previous step).

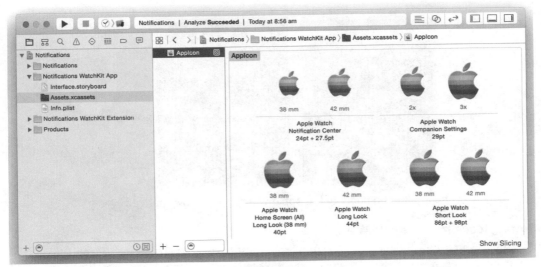

Figure 8.13   Setting the icons for the project

3. In the Interface.storyboard file, observe that the Static Interface Controller and Dynamic Interface Controller now display the icons (see Figure 8.14).

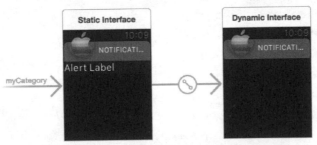

Figure 8.14   The Interface Controllers now show the icon

4. Run the application on the iPhone Simulator. You should now see the icon on the Static Interface Controller (see Figure 8.15).

Figure 8.15   The icon showing on the Static Interface Controller

Setting Background Images

You can also display a background image on the Static Interface Controller:

1. Drag and drop an image named background.png onto the Assets.xcassets file (in the WatchKit app; see Figure 8.16). Be sure to move it into the 2× box in the Apple Watch section.

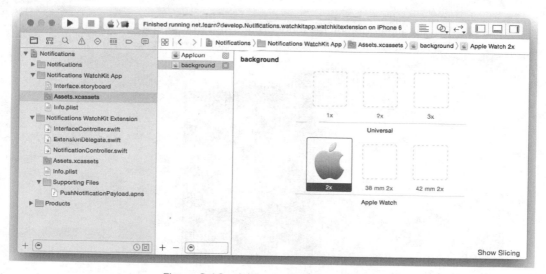

Figure 8.16   Adding an image to the project

2. Select the Static Interface Controller in the Interface.storyboard file and set its Background attribute to **background** (see Figure 8.17). Also, set its Mode attribute to **Aspect Fit**.

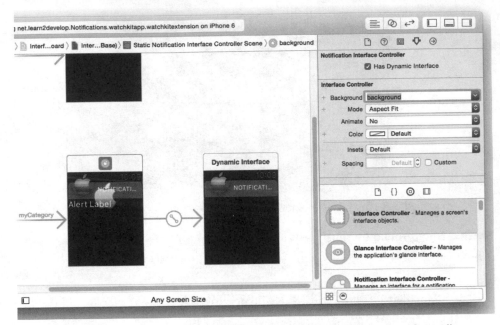

Figure 8.17   Setting the background image for the Static Interface Controller

3. Run the application on the iPhone Simulator. You should now see the background image on the Static Interface Controller (see Figure 8.18).

Figure 8.18   The background image on
the Static Interface Controller

Action Buttons

Earlier, you saw that the PushNotificationPayload.apns file contains the payload of a remote notification. In the WatchKit Simulator Actions key, you saw that you have a single item titled `First Button` with the identifier of `firstButtonAction`:

```
"WatchKit Simulator Actions": [
    {
        "title": "First Button",
        "identifier": "firstButtonAction"
    }
],
```

This item simulates that your remote notification contains a single action button. The `title` key contains the title of the button to display in the short-look interface, and the `identifier` key contains the ID of the button that you can programmatically reference when the button is tapped.

You can simulate your remote notification containing multiple action buttons:

1. Modify/add the following statements in bold to the PushNotificationPayload.apns file:

```
{
    "aps": {
        "alert": {
            "body":
            "Boarding Now\nFlight 164 to Los Angeles boards at 6:50AM at
            Gate 46",
            "title": "Boarding"
        },
        "category": "myCategory"
    },

    "WatchKit Simulator Actions": [
        {
            "title": "Itinerary",
            "identifier": "btnItinerary"
        },
        {
            "title": "Weather",
            "identifier": "btnWeather",
        },
        {
            "title": "Cancel Boarding",
            "identifier": "btnCancel",
            "destructive": 1
        },
    ],
```

```
        "customKey": "Use this file to define a testing payload for your
    notifications. The aps dictionary specifies the category, alert text, and
    title. The WatchKit Simulator Actions array can provide info for one or
    more action buttons in addition to the standard Dismiss button. Any other
    top level keys are custom payload. If you have multiple such JSON files
    in your project, you'll be able to select them when choosing to debug the
    notification interface of your Watch App."
    }
```

The `destructive` key with a value of 1 indicates that this action button is a destructive one.

2. Run the application on the iPhone Simulator. Observe that the short-look interface now displays four buttons (including the **Dismiss** button), with the destructive action button displayed in red (see Figure 8.19).

Figure 8.19   The Static Interface Controller displaying four buttons

> **Note**
>
> Realistically, the short-look interface is short-lived—the user does not have much time to look at the screen and tap the buttons before the short-look interface transitions to the long-look interface.

Handling the Action Buttons

As described at the beginning of this chapter, a notification can contain action buttons. There are two types of action buttons: foreground and background. When a notification is received and displayed on the iPhone, a foreground action button launches the iPhone application and brings it to the foreground, whereas a background action button launches the iPhone application and executes in the background.

On the Apple Watch,

- A foreground action button fires either the `handleActionWithIdentifier:-forLocalNotification:` (for local notifications) or `handleActionWith-Identifier:forRemoteNotification:` (for remote notifications) method of the main Interface Controller for your Watch app.

- A background action button fires either the `application:handleAction-WithIdentifier:forLocalNotification:` (for local notifications) or the `application:handleActionWithIdentifier:forRemoteNotification:` (for remote notifications) method in the containing iOS app.

1. In the Interface.storyboard file, add two Label controls onto the Interface Controller (see Figure 8.20). Set the Lines attributes of both Label controls to **0**.

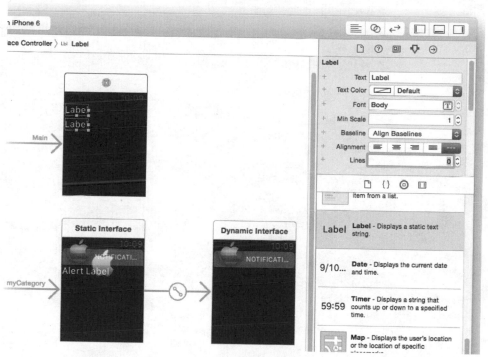

Figure 8.20   Adding two Label controls to the Interface Controller

2. Create two outlets for the Label controls. This adds the following statements in bold to the InterfaceController.swift file:

```
import WatchKit
import Foundation

class InterfaceController: WKInterfaceController {

    @IBOutlet var label1: WKInterfaceLabel!
    @IBOutlet var label2: WKInterfaceLabel!
```

```
override func awakeWithContext(context: AnyObject?) {
    super.awakeWithContext(context)

    // Configure interface objects here.
}
```

3. In the PushNotificationPayload.apns file, add the following statements in bold:

```
{
    "aps": {
        "alert": {
            "body":
            "Boarding Now\nFlight 164 to Los Angeles boards at 6:50AM at
              Gate 46",
            "title": "Boarding"
        },
        "category": "myCategory"
    },

    "WatchKit Simulator Actions": [
        {
            "title": "Itinerary",
            "identifier": "btnItinerary"
        },
        {
            "title": "Weather",
            "identifier": "btnWeather",
        },
        {
            "title": "Cancel Boarding",
            "identifier": "btnCancel",
            "destructive": 1
        },
    ],

    "gateclose":"7:30AM",

    "customKey": "Use this file to define a testing payload for your
    notifications. The aps dictionary specifies the category, alert text, and
    title. The WatchKit Simulator Actions array can provide info for one or
    more action buttons in addition to the standard Dismiss button. Any other
    top level keys are custom payload. If you have multiple such JSON files
    in your project, you'll be able to select them when choosing to debug the
    notification interface of your Watch App."
}
```

4. Add the following statements in bold to the InterfaceController.swift file:

```
import WatchKit
import Foundation
```

```
class InterfaceController: WKInterfaceController {

    @IBOutlet var label1: WKInterfaceLabel!
    @IBOutlet var label2: WKInterfaceLabel!

    override func awakeWithContext(context: AnyObject?) {
        super.awakeWithContext(context)

        // Configure interface objects here.
        label1.setText("")
        label2.setText("")
    }

    func handleButtons (btnIdentifier : String) {

        switch btnIdentifier {
        case "btnItinerary":
            label2.setText("Arriving in Los Angeles at 11:50AM")
        case "btnWeather":
            label2.setText("The weather in Los Angeles is 62 degrees")
        case "btnCancel":
            label2.setText("Please proceed to the gate immediately.")
        default:break
        }
    }

    //---fired when a foreground action button in a local notification
    // is tapped---
    override func handleActionWithIdentifier(identifier: String?,
        forLocalNotification localNotification: UILocalNotification) {
        handleButtons(identifier!)
    }

    //---fired when a foreground action button in a remote notification
    // is tapped---
    override func handleActionWithIdentifier(identifier: String?,
    forRemoteNotification remoteNotification: [NSObject : AnyObject]) {
        if let s = remoteNotification["gateclose"] as? String {
            label1.setText("Gate Close: \(s)")
        }
        handleButtons(identifier!)
    }
}
```

The first argument of the handleActionWithIdentifier:forRemote-
Notification: method passes in the identifier of the action button. The second
argument passes in a copy of the notification received. Here, you can retrieve the
content and use it to get the time the gate closes.

> **Note**
>
> The main entry point for your watch application (which is of type `WKInterface-Controller`) handles all foreground actions of the notifications. The handling is not performed at the Notification Controller.

5. Run the application on the iPhone Simulator and click one of the buttons shown on the Apple Watch Simulator (see Figure 8.21). You should see the main Interface Controller launch, showing the details of the notification.

Figure 8.21   Clicking any action button launches the default
Interface Controller on the watch app

6. For background actions, you need to implement the `application:handleAction-WithIdentifier:forLocalNotification:` and the `application:handle-ActionWithIdentifier:forRemoteNotification:` methods in the containing iOS app. Add the following statements in bold to the AppDelegate.swift file:

```
import UIKit

@UIApplicationMain
class AppDelegate: UIResponder, UIApplicationDelegate {

    var window: UIWindow?

    func handleButtons (btnIdentifier : String) {
        //...
    }

    //---fired when a background action button in a local notification
    // is tapped---
    func application(application: UIApplication,
        handleActionWithIdentifier identifier: String?,
        forLocalNotification notification: UILocalNotification,
```

```
            completionHandler: () -> Void) {
            handleButtons(identifier!)
    }

    //---fired when a background action button in a remote notification
    // is tapped---
    func application(application: UIApplication,
            handleActionWithIdentifier identifier: String?,
            forRemoteNotification userInfo: [NSObject : AnyObject],
            completionHandler: () -> Void) {
            handleButtons(identifier!)
    }
```

> **Note**
>
> You can test this code only on an actual iOS device and Apple Watch.

Implementing the Long-Look Interface

When the user taps the short-look interface or keeps his or her wrist raised, the long-look interface appears. The long-look interface allows you to display the notification in more detail (such as using additional Label and Image controls). However, interactions with the user are still not allowed, apart from the action buttons and the **Dismiss** button. This means that you cannot add your own Button control to the long-look interface. The following steps show you how to implement the long-look interface:

1. Add the following statements in bold to the PushNotificationPayload.apns file:

```
{
    "aps": {
        "alert": {
            "body":
            "Boarding Now\nFlight 164 to Los Angeles boards at 6:50AM at
              Gate 46",
            "title": "Boarding"
        },
        "category": "myCategory"
    },

    "WatchKit Simulator Actions": [
        {
            "title": "Itinerary",
            "identifier": "btnItinerary"
        },
        {
            "title": "Weather",
            "identifier": "btnWeather",
        },
```

```
        {
            "title": "Cancel Boarding",
            "identifier": "btnCancel",
            "destructive": 1
        },
    ],

    "gateclose":"7:30AM",
    "status":"Boarding",
    "flight":"164",
    "time":"6:50AM",
    "gate":"46",
    "customKey": "Use this file to define a testing payload for your
notifications. The aps dictionary specifies the category, alert text, and
title. The WatchKit Simulator Actions array can provide info for one or
more action buttons in addition to the standard Dismiss button. Any other
top level keys are custom payload. If you have multiple such JSON files
in your project, you'll be able to select them when choosing to debug the
notification interface of your Watch App."
}
```

The previous statements simulate the notification containing the additional information about a particular flight.

2. In the Interface.storyboard file, add an Image control and three Label controls to the Dynamic Interface Controller (see Figure 8.22). For each of the four controls, set the Horizontal attribute to **Center**. Also, set the Lines attribute for each of the Label controls to **0**.

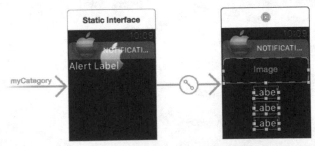

Figure 8.22   Adding four controls to the Dynamic Interface Controller

3. Drag and drop two images named boarding.png and info.png into the Assets.xcassets file located in the WatchKit app (see Figure 8.23).

4. Examine the Dynamic Interface Controller and observe from its Identity Inspector window that its Class is set to NotificationController (see Figure 8.24). This class is represented by the NotificationController.swift file located in the Extension project.

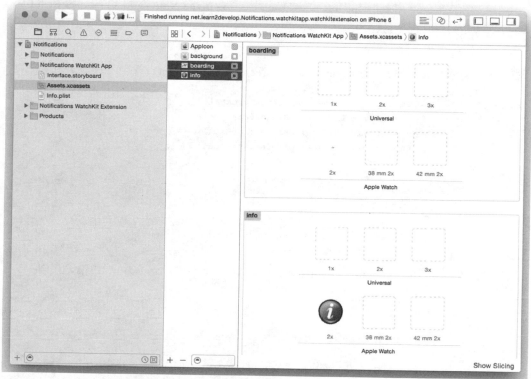

Figure 8.23   Adding more images to the WatchKit app project

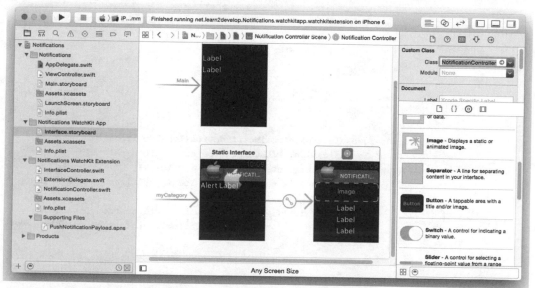

Figure 8.24   The class representing the Dynamic Interface Controller

5. Create outlets for the Image and Label controls in the NotificationController.swift file:

```
import WatchKit
import Foundation

class NotificationController: WKUserNotificationInterfaceController {

    @IBOutlet var image: WKInterfaceImage!
    @IBOutlet var lblBody: WKInterfaceLabel!
    @IBOutlet var lblGate: WKInterfaceLabel!
    @IBOutlet var lblTime: WKInterfaceLabel!

    override init() {
        // Initialize variables here.
        super.init()

        // Configure interface objects here.
    }
```

6. Add the following statements in bold to the NotificationController.swift file:

```
import WatchKit
import Foundation

class NotificationController: WKUserNotificationInterfaceController {

    @IBOutlet var image: WKInterfaceImage!
    @IBOutlet var lblBody: WKInterfaceLabel!
    @IBOutlet var lblGate: WKInterfaceLabel!
    @IBOutlet var lblTime: WKInterfaceLabel!

    override init() {
        // Initialize variables here.
        super.init()

        // Configure interface objects here.
    }

    override func didReceiveLocalNotification(localNotification:
        UILocalNotification, withCompletion completionHandler:
        ((WKUserNotificationInterfaceType) -> Void)) {
            // This method is called when a local notification needs to be
            // presented.
            // Implement it if you use a dynamic notification interface.
            // Populate your dynamic notification interface as quickly as
            // possible.
            //
```

```
        // After populating your dynamic notification interface call the
        // completion block.
        completionHandler(.Custom)
    }

    override func didReceiveRemoteNotification(remoteNotification:
        [NSObject : AnyObject], withCompletion completionHandler:
        ((WKUserNotificationInterfaceType) -> Void)) {
        // This method is called when a remote notification needs to be
        // presented.
        // Implement it if you use a dynamic notification interface.
        // Populate your dynamic notification interface as quickly as
        // possible.
        //
        // After populating your dynamic notification interface call the
        // completion block.


        let alert = remoteNotification["aps"]!["alert"]! as! NSDictionary
        self.lblBody.setText(alert["body"]! as? String)

        if remoteNotification["status"] as! String == "Boarding" {
            self.image.setImageNamed("boarding")
        } else if remoteNotification["status"] as! String == "Delayed" {
            self.image.setImageNamed("info")
        }

        self.lblGate.setText("Gate: " +
            (remoteNotification["gate"] as! String))
        self.lblTime.setText("Boarding: " + (remoteNotification["time"]
            as! String))
        completionHandler(.Custom)
    }
}
```

To implement the long-look interface, you need to implement the following two methods in the NotificationController class:

- didReceiveLocalNotification:withCompletion: is fired when a local notification is received.

- didReceiveRemoteNotification:withCompletion: is fired when a remote notification is received.

In both methods, you should perform your task quickly. If they take a long time to execute, the Apple Watch will default back to the short-look interface. At the end of the method, you have to call the completion handler, completionHandler, by passing it an enumeration of type WKUserNotificationInterfaceType.

Typically, you use `Custom`, but you can also use `Default` to default back to the short-look interface if the payload does not contain what you expected.

Because the Apple Watch Simulator simulates only remote notification, add the code in the `didReceiveRemoteNotification:withCompletion:` method to extract the flight details from the notification payload and display the extra details on the Image and Label controls.

> **Note**
>
> For testing on the Apple Simulator, if you implement the `didReceiveRemoteNotification:withCompletion:` method and return `Custom` for the completion handler, the Dynamic Interface Controller is displayed when you run the app on the iPhone Simulator. Otherwise, the Static Interface Controller always loads.

7. Run the application on the iPhone Simulator. You should now see the long-look interface showing the icon and the details of the flight (see Figure 8.25).

Figure 8.25   The Dynamic Interface Controller showing the details of the flight

Simulating Using Different Notification Payloads

Besides the default PushNotificationPayload.apns file included in the Extension project for simulating a remote notification, you can also add files to simulate additional remote notifications:

1. Right-click the **Supporting Files** group of the Extension and add a new file. Select **iOS | Apple Watch | Notification Simulation File** (see Figure 8.26) and click **Next**. Name the file **NotificationPayload-delayed**. The file should now appear in the Supporting Files group (see Figure 8.27).

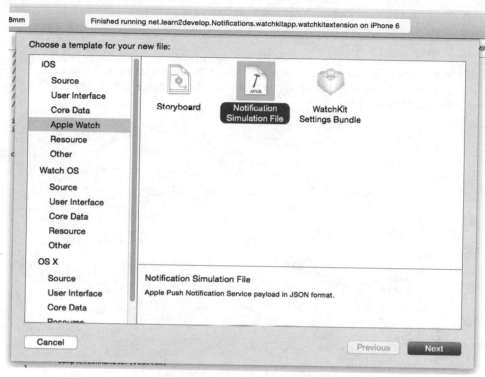

Figure 8.26   Adding a Notification Simulation File to the project

Figure 8.27   The newly added payload file

2. Populate the NotificationPayload–delayed.apns file as follows:

> **Note**
>
> The value of the `body` key in the NotificationPayload-delayed.apns file has been formatted for readability. When testing on the iPhone Simulator, it should be a continuous line: "Flight Delayed\nFlight 164 to Los Angeles now boards at 7:50AM at Gate 56."

```
{
    "aps": {
        "alert": {
            "body": "Flight Delayed\nFlight 164 to Los Angeles now
                     boards at 7:50AM at Gate 56",
            "title": "Apple Air"
        },
        "category": "myCategory"
    },

    "status": "Delayed",
    "flight" :"164",
    "time": "7:50AM",
    "gate": "56",
    "gateclose":"8:30AM",

    "WatchKit Simulator Actions": [
        {
            "title": "Itinerary",
            "identifier": "btnItinerary"
        },
        {
            "title": "Weather",
            "identifier": "btnWeather",
        },
        {

            "title": "Cancel Boarding",
            "identifier": "btnCancel",
            "destructive": 1
        },
    ]
}
```

3. To select the newly added payload file for testing, select the **Edit Scheme...** item located at the top of Xcode (see Figure 8.28).

Figure 8.28   Editing the scheme to run the project

4. In the Run configuration, select **NotificationPayload–delayed.apns** as the Notification Payload (see Figure 8.29).

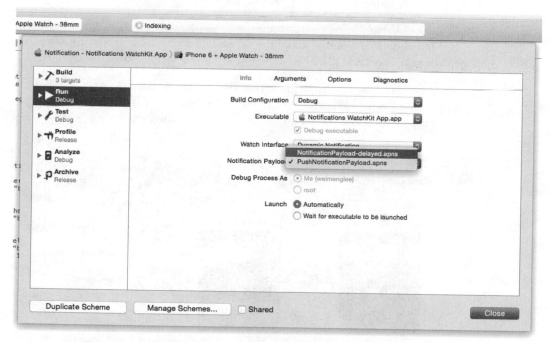

Figure 8.29   Choosing the new payload file for simulating a notification

5. Run the application on the iPhone Simulator. You should now see the long-look interface showing a different set of icons and details of the flight (see Figure 8.30).

Figure 8.30 The Dynamic Interface Controller showing the details of the new notification

Changing Sash Color

Both the Static Interface Controller and the Dynamic Interface Controller allow you to change their sash colors and title colors:

1. Select the **myCategory** arrow in the Interface.storyboard file and, in the Attributes Inspector window, change its Sash Color to **Yellow** and Title Color to **Blue** (see Figure 8.31). You should immediately see the changes in color.

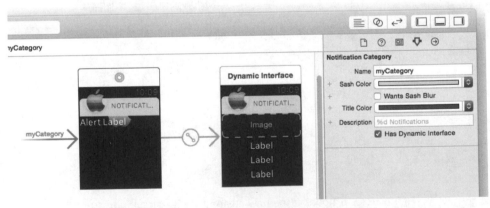

Figure 8.31 Changing the sash and title colors

2. Run the application on the iPhone Simulator, and observe the sash and title colors in the Dynamic Interface Controller (see Figure 8.32).

Figure 8.32   The sash and title
colors are now changed

Summary

In this chapter, you learned how to implement notifications in your Apple Watch apps.
You learned about the different types of notifications and how they are handled in the
Apple Watch. You also saw how to simulate notifications with different payloads. In the
next chapter, you learn how to implement glances in your Apple Watch apps.

Displaying Glances

Every good product I've ever seen is because a group of people cared deeply about making something wonderful that they and their friends wanted. They wanted to use it themselves.

Steve Jobs

Most people interact with their watches by *glancing* at the watch to check the time. For the Apple Watch, Apple has extended this traditional form of interaction by providing glances for your watch applications. Instead of just glancing for the time, users can have a quick glance at the state of the various applications. Glances are shown when users swipe up on the watch. The Apple Watch then shows a scrollable list of glances from apps that support them (up to a maximum of 20 glances). Think of glances as snapshots of the various apps on the watch: Instagram may show the most recently shared photo, and Twitter may show the latest trending tweets. Glances provide users with a quick summary of information that may be important to them. If a user wants more details, tapping a glance launches the corresponding watch app.

If your app supports glances, you need to add a Glance scene to your storyboard file. Each user needs to manually turn on the glance of your application through the Apple Watch application on the watch.

In this chapter, you learn how to implement glances for your watch apps.

What Is a Glance?

From a developer's perspective, a glance is an additional avenue for your app to display a quick summary of information to the user. Imagine an iPhone app that fetches stock prices at regular time intervals. A user who wants to have a quick look at the price of a particular stock can simply swipe up on the watch face and view the most recently fetched price of the stock. This can be done without launching your app. Of course, if the user wants to view more detailed information, he or she can tap the glance to launch the app. One noteworthy feature of glances is that users have no way of interacting with them—there are no controls for users to interact with. They are solely for the purpose of showing information quickly to the users, hence the name.

Implementing Glances

Let's look at how to implement a glance for an application:

1. Using Xcode, create a new iOS App with WatchKit App project and name it
   DisplayingGlances. For this project, uncheck the Include Notification Scene
   option and check the Include Glance Scene option (see Figure 9.1).

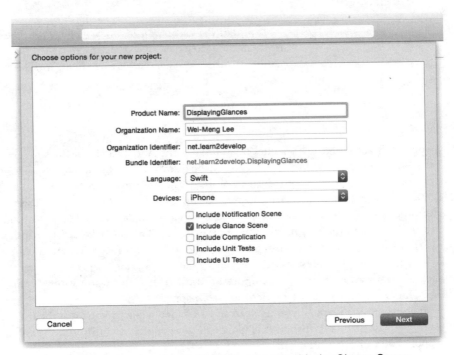

Figure 9.1   Adding the WatchKit App target with the Glance Scene

2. In the WatchKit app, select the Interface.storyboard file. You should now see the
   Glance Interface Controller together with the Interface Controller (see Figure 9.2).

   Note

   Each watch app can contain at most one Glance Interface Controller.

3. In the Extension project, you see the GlanceController.swift file (see Figure 9.3).

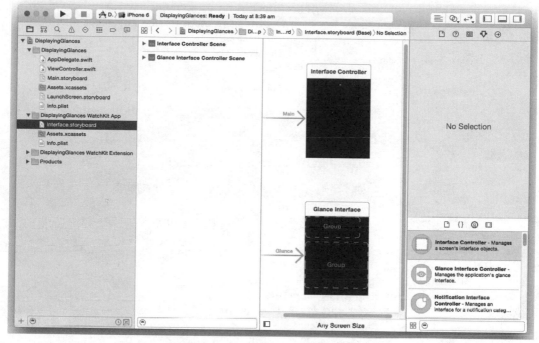

Figure 9.2   The Glance Interface Controller together with the Interface Controller

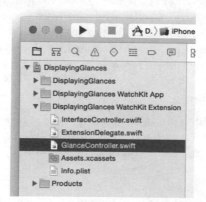

Figure 9.3   The GlanceController.swift file
in the Extension project

4. The GlanceController.swift file contains the `GlanceController` class, which represents the Glance Interface Controller in the Interface.storyboard file:

```
import WatchKit
import Foundation

class GlanceController: WKInterfaceController {

    override func awakeWithContext(context: AnyObject?) {
        super.awakeWithContext(context)

        // Configure interface objects here.
    }

    override func willActivate() {
        // This method is called when watch view controller is about
        // to be visible to user.
        super.willActivate()
    }

    override func didDeactivate() {
        // This method is called when watch view controller is no longer visible.
        super.didDeactivate()
    }

}
```

Observe that the `GlanceController` class extends the `WKInterfaceController` class, the same as the Interface Controller. The same Interface Controller lifecycle applies to the Glance Controller as well. The only exception is that for a Glance Controller, the initialization takes place very early so that the information can be quickly displayed. Hence, you should try to update your glances in the `willActivate` method.

Customizing the Glance

Glances can be customized to display different types of information. However, as with notifications, users are not allowed to have interactions with the glances. This means that controls, like Button and Slider controls, are not allowed.

> **Note**
>
> Remember that glances are supposed to show users information quickly. Hence, you should design your glances to convey as much relevant information as quickly as possible.

1. Select the Glance Interface Controller in the Interface.storyboard file and view its Attributes Inspector window (see Figure 9.4). Observe that it is divided into two sections: Upper and Lower. Both contain the Group control, which allows you to add controls like labels and images.

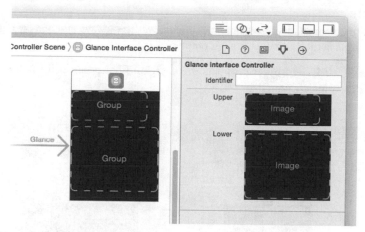

Figure 9.4   The Glance Interface Controller is divided into two sections

2. Click the **Upper** group in the Attributes Inspector window, and you see a popover list (see Figure 9.5). This is a list of predefined templates for some of the common designs for the Upper section. Select the bottom-left item.

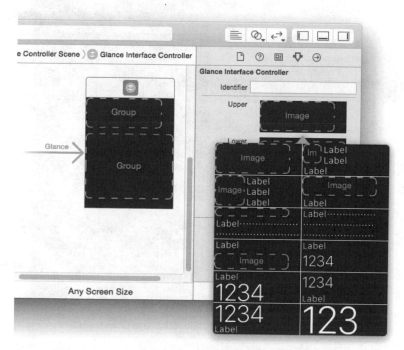

Figure 9.5   Selecting the template for the Upper section

> **Note**
>
> If you do not like the predefined templates, you can always add and lay out your own controls in the Glance Interface Controller.

3. Likewise, click the **Lower** group, and you see another popover list (see Figure 9.6). Select the top-left item.

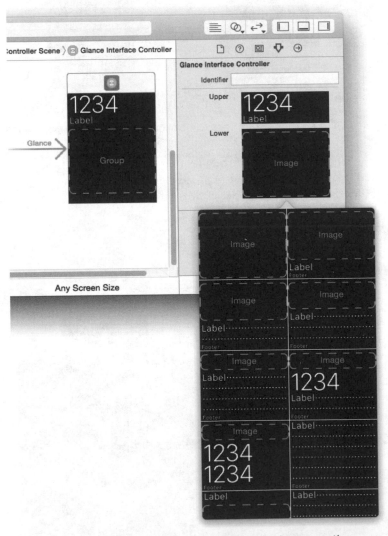

Figure 9.6   Selecting the template for the Lower section

4. Add a Label control to the Lower group (see Figure 9.7) and set its attributes as follows:

> Font: **System Italic**
>
> Size: **30**
>
> Text Color: **Yellow**
>
> Style: **Bold**
>
> Horizontal: **Center**
>
> Vertical: **Center**

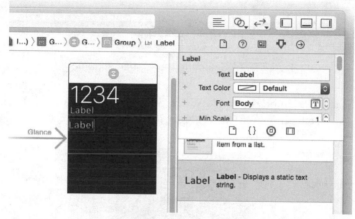

Figure 9.7   Adding a Label control to the Lower section

Note

You can only use the system font (San Francisco) for glances and notifications on the Apple Watch; custom fonts are not supported.

5. The Glance Interface Controller now looks like Figure 9.8.

Figure 9.8   The final design for the Glance Interface Controller

Testing the Glance

To test the glance, you need to use the Glance scheme that was created in Xcode when you added the WatchKit App target:

1. In Xcode, select the **Glance – DisplayingGlances WatchKit App** scheme (see Figure 9.9) and then select **iPhone 6 + Apple Watch – 38mm**.

Figure 9.9   Selecting the Glance scheme

2. Run the application on the Apple Watch Simulator. You now see the glance on the Apple Watch Simulator (see Figure 9.10).

Figure 9.10   Displaying the glance on the
Apple Watch Simulator

At this moment, the glance is not doing anything useful. In the next section, you modify the application to display some useful information.

Making the Glance Useful

To make the glance display useful information, you must modify the containing iOS application to perform a background fetch. Your iOS app can then perform a network operation even if it is switched to the background.

In the background fetch, the iOS app connects to a Yahoo web service to fetch the prices of two stocks: AAPL (Apple) and MSFT (Microsoft). Once the prices of the two stocks are fetched, the price of AAPL is sent to the Apple Watch using the `ApplicationContext` method in the Watch Connectivity Framework (covered in Chapter 7, "Interfacing with iOS Apps"). (For this example, you send the price of only one stock even though you also downloaded the price of MSFT.)

- In the watch app, the values received from the iPhone are saved using the `NSUserDefaults` settings.

- Whenever the glance is shown, the values of the stocks are retrieved from the `NSUserDefaults` settings and then displayed.

Implementing Background Fetch

The containing iOS app connects to the Yahoo web service and downloads the stock prices of Apple and Microsoft when the application is in the background.

1. To implement background fetch on the containing iOS app, select the **Displaying-Glances** target in Xcode and, in the Capabilities tab, check the Background fetch option under the Background Modes section (see Figure 9.11).

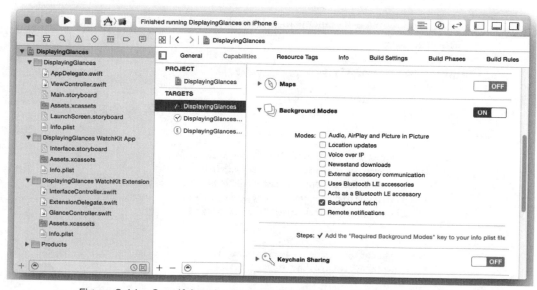

Figure 9.11   Specifying the background fetch capability for the iOS app

2. In the Info.plist file in the iOS project, add the two keys `NSAppTransportSecurity` and `NSAllowsArbitraryLoads`, as shown in Figure 9.12. These two keys are needed so that you can connect to a web server using `http://` instead of `https://` (which is the default).

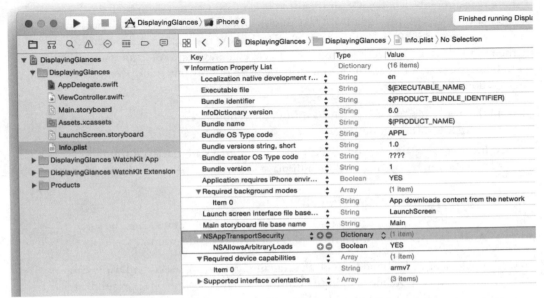

Figure 9.12   Adding the keys in Info.plist to enable `http://`

3. Add the following statements in bold to the AppDelegate.swift file:

```
import UIKit

import WatchConnectivity

@UIApplicationMain
class AppDelegate: UIResponder, UIApplicationDelegate, WCSessionDelegate {
    var window: UIWindow?

    //---convert from NSDate format to String---
    func currentDateToString() -> String {
        let formatter: NSDateFormatter = NSDateFormatter()
        formatter.dateFormat = "yyyy-MM-dd HH:mm:ss zzz"
        return formatter.stringFromDate(NSDate())
    }

    //---extract the required data from the JSON string---
    func parseJSONData(data: NSData) {
        do {
            let parsedJSONData =
            try NSJSONSerialization.JSONObjectWithData(data,
                options: NSJSONReadingOptions()) as!
                [String:AnyObject]
```

```swift
        let query = parsedJSONData["query"] as!
            [String:AnyObject]
        if let results = query["results"] as?
            [String:AnyObject] {
            if let quotes = results["quote"] as?
                [[String:AnyObject]] {
                for stock in quotes {
                    let symbol = stock["symbol"] as! String
                    let ask = stock["Ask"] as! String
                    let lastupdate = currentDateToString()

                    //---debugging---
                    print(symbol)
                    print(ask)
                    print(lastupdate)

                    if symbol == "AAPL" {
                        do {
                            let applicationContext = [
                                "symbol" : symbol,
                                "lastupdate" : lastupdate,
                                "ask": ask]
                            try
                                WCSession.defaultSession().
                                    updateApplicationContext(
                                        applicationContext)
                        } catch {
                            print("\(error)")
                        }
                    }
                }
            }
        }
    } catch {
        print(error)
    }
}


//---performing a background fetch---
func application(application: UIApplication,
    performFetchWithCompletionHandler completionHandler:
    (UIBackgroundFetchResult) -> Void) {

    /*

        For http://, you need to add the following keys in
        info.plist:
        NSAppTransportSecurity
```

```
        NSAllowsArbitraryLoads - YES
        Application Transport Security has blocked a cleartext
            HTTP (http://) resource load since it is insecure.
            Temporary exceptions can be configured via your app's
            Info.plist file.
    */

    let urlString =
        "http://query.yahooapis.com/v1/public/yql?q=" +
        "select%20*%20from%20yahoo.finance.quotes%20" +
        "where%20symbol%20in%20(%22AAPL%22%2C%22MSFT%22)" +
        "%0A%09%09&env=http%3A%2F%2Fdatatables.org%2" +
        "Falltables.env&format=json"

    let session = NSURLSession.sharedSession()
    session.dataTaskWithURL(NSURL(string:urlString)!,
    completionHandler: {
        (data, response, error) -> Void in
        let httpResp = response as! NSHTTPURLResponse
        if error == nil && httpResp.statusCode == 200 {
            //---parse the JSON result---
            self.parseJSONData(data!)
            completionHandler(UIBackgroundFetchResult.NewData)
        } else {
            completionHandler(UIBackgroundFetchResult.Failed)
        }
    }).resume()
}


func application(application: UIApplication,
    didFinishLaunchingWithOptions launchOptions:
    [NSObject: AnyObject]?) -> Bool {

    // Override point for customization after application launch.

    if (WCSession.isSupported()) {
        let session = WCSession.defaultSession()
        session.delegate = self
        session.activateSession()
    }

    return true
}
```

> **Note**
> Remember to change the shared group name to the one that you have used.

You just enabled the following to happen:

- You connect to the Yahoo web service to fetch the price of Apple and Microsoft.
- The web service returns the result as a JSON string.
- You pass the JSON string to the `parseJSONData:` method to extract the relevant data: stock symbol and asking price.
- The `currentDateToString` method returns the current date and time as a `String` object.
- The stock symbols, asking prices, and the date and time the prices were fetched are sent to the Apple Watch using the `ApplicationContext` method.

4. Select the **DisplayingGlances** scheme (see Figure 9.13) in Xcode and run the application on the iPhone Simulator.

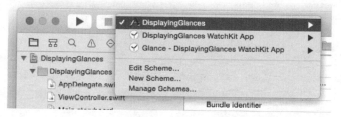

Figure 9.13   Selecting the **DisplayingGlances** scheme

5. To simulate a background fetch on the application, select **Debug | Simulate Background Fetch** in Xcode. If the stock prices are downloaded correctly, you should now see the prices in the Output window (see Figure 9.14).

```
AAPL
106.30
2015-08-24 12:46:15 GMT+8
MSFT
43.46
2015-08-24 12:46:15 GMT+8
```

Figure 9.14   The stock prices downloaded
from the web service

Updating the Glance

Now that the stock prices are downloaded and saved, you can display them on the Glance Interface Controller:

1. In the GlanceController.swift file, create three outlets for the three Label controls in the Glance Interface Controller:

```swift
import WatchKit
import Foundation
```

```
class GlanceController: WKInterfaceController {

    @IBOutlet var lblSymbol: WKInterfaceLabel!

    @IBOutlet var lblLastUpdate: WKInterfaceLabel!

    @IBOutlet var lblAsk: WKInterfaceLabel!

    override func awakeWithContext(context: AnyObject?) {
        super.awakeWithContext(context)

        // Configure interface objects here.
    }
```

2. Add the following statements in bold to the GlanceController.swift file:

```
import WatchKit
import Foundation

import WatchConnectivity

class GlanceController: WKInterfaceController, WCSessionDelegate {
    @IBOutlet var lblSymbol: WKInterfaceLabel!

    @IBOutlet var lblLastUpdate: WKInterfaceLabel!

    @IBOutlet var lblAsk: WKInterfaceLabel!

    override func awakeWithContext(context: AnyObject?) {
        super.awakeWithContext(context)

        // Configure interface objects here.
        if (WCSession.isSupported()) {
            let session = WCSession.defaultSession()
            session.delegate = self
            session.activateSession()
        }
    }

    func session(session: WCSession, didReceiveApplicationContext
        applicationContext: [String : AnyObject]) {
        let defaults = NSUserDefaults.standardUserDefaults()
        defaults.setValue(applicationContext["symbol"]! as! String,
            forKey: "symbol")
        defaults.setValue(applicationContext["lastupdate"]! as! String,
            forKey: "lastupdate")
```

```swift
    defaults.setValue(applicationContext["ask"]! as! String,
        forKey: "ask")
    defaults.synchronize()
}


//---convert from string to NSDate---
func dateStringToDate(date:String) -> NSDate {
    let dateFormatter = NSDateFormatter()
    dateFormatter.dateFormat = "yyyy-MM-dd HH:mm:ss zzz"
    return dateFormatter.dateFromString(date)!
}


override func willActivate() {
    // This method is called when watch view controller is about to
    // be visible to user.
    super.willActivate()

    let defaults = NSUserDefaults.standardUserDefaults()

    if defaults.valueForKey("lastupdate") != nil {
        //---retrieve the price and date fetched from the settings---
        let lastupdate = dateStringToDate(
            (defaults.valueForKey("lastupdate") as? String)!)
        let price = defaults.valueForKey("ask") as? String
        let symbol = defaults.valueForKey("symbol") as? String

        //---the difference between the current time and the time the
        // price was fetched---
        let elapsedTime = NSDate().timeIntervalSinceDate(lastupdate)

        //---convert to seconds---
        let elapsedTimeSeconds = Int(elapsedTime)

        //---convert the time to mins and secs---
        let elapsedMin = elapsedTimeSeconds / 60
        let elapsedSec = elapsedTimeSeconds % 60

        if elapsedMin > 0 {
            lblLastUpdate.setText(
                "\(elapsedMin) mins \(Int(elapsedSec)) secs")
        } else {
            lblLastUpdate.setText("\(Int(elapsedTime)) secs")
        }
        //---show the info on the glance---
        self.lblSymbol.setText(symbol)
        self.lblAsk.setText("$" + price!)
    }
}
```

You just enabled the following to happen:

- When the Glance Controller is awakened, you want to activate the session for the Watch Connectivity Framework so that you can receive the incoming stock information sent from the watch.

- You load the values saved in the NSUserDefaults settings. For simplicity, you are retrieving only one stock price: AAPL. The value of the AAPL key is a dictionary containing the price as well as the date and time it was fetched.

- The dateStringToDate: method accepts the date and time as a String and then returns an NSDate object.

- You calculate the elapsed time since the price was fetched using the timeIntervalSinceDate: method of the NSDate object.

- You then display the stock symbol, the elapsed time since the price was fetched, and the price of the stock in the Glance Interface Controller.

3. In Xcode, switch to the **Glance – DisplayingGlances WatchKit App** scheme and test the application on the iPhone Simulator. The Glance Interface Controller should now look like Figure 9.15.

Figure 9.15   The glance showing the
latest fetched price

Summary

In this chapter, you learned how to implement glances in your Apple Watch application. You also learned how to perform background fetch in your containing iOS application and then display the information downloaded in your Glance Interface Controller.

Index

REGISTER YOUR PRODUCT at informit.com/register

Access Additional Benefits and SAVE 35% on Your Next Purchase

- Download available product updates.

- Access bonus material when applicable.

- Receive exclusive offers on new editions and related products.
  (Just check the box to hear from us when setting up your account.)

- Get a coupon for 35% for your next purchase, valid for 30 days. Your code will be available in your InformIT cart. (You will also find it in the Manage Codes section of your account page.)

Registration benefits vary by product. Benefits will be listed on your account page under Registered Products.

InformIT.com—The Trusted Technology Learning Source

InformIT is the online home of information technology brands at Pearson, the world's foremost education company. At InformIT.com you can

- Shop our books, eBooks, software, and video training.
- Take advantage of our special offers and promotions (informit.com/promotions).
- Sign up for special offers and content newsletters (informit.com/newsletters).
- Read free articles and blogs by information technology experts.
- Access thousands of free chapters and video lessons.

Connect with InformIT—Visit informit.com/community

Learn about InformIT community events and programs.

the trusted technology learning source

Addison-Wesley · Cisco Press · IBM Press · Microsoft Press · Pearson IT Certification · Prentice Hall · Que · Sams · VMware Press